ASSEMBLY REQUIRED

HOW TO HYPERSCALE YOUR SALES, DOMINATE THE COMPETITION, AND BECOME THE MARKET LEADER

DONALD SCHERER

AN INC.
ORIGINAL

An Inc. Original
New York, New York
www.inc.com

This work is being published under the *An Inc. Original* imprint by an exclusive
arrangement with *Inc. Magazine. Inc. Magazine* and the *Inc.* logo are registered
trademarks of Mansueto Ventures, LLC. The *An Inc. Original* logo is a wholly
owned trademark of Mansueto Ventures, LLC.

Distributed by Greenleaf Book Group

For ordering information or special discounts for bulk purchases, please contact
Greenleaf Book Group at PO Box 91869, Austin, TX 78709, 512.891.6100.

Design and composition by Greenleaf Book Group and Kim Lance
Cover design by Greenleaf Book Group and Kim Lance
Cover images ©Epifantsev/Thinkstock and ©Jacky Co/Shutterstock.com

Cataloging-in-Publication data is available.

Print ISBN: 978-1-62634-412-9

eBook ISBN: 978-1-62634-413-6

Part of the Tree Neutral® program, which offsets the number of trees consumed in
the production and printing of this book by taking proactive steps, such as planting
trees in direct proportion to the number of trees used: www.treeneutral.com

TreeNeutral®

Printed in the United States of America on acid-free paper

17 18 19 20 21 22   10 9 8 7 6 5 4 3 2 1

First Edition

To the members of the original CrossBorder Solutions management team, including Joe Mileti, Dave Bukovac, Scott Miller, Stephanie Israel, and Jeff Mattes, my sincerest thanks for helping me develop our sales assembly line. Without your constant contributions, the experiment never would have worked!

Finally, my love and appreciation goes to my family, especially my mother, Joan Scherer, for being my codeveloper in advancing all the ideas behind the sales assembly line methodology and building the sales automation software that drove CrossBorder Solutions' success.

CONTENTS **A.R.**

What This Book Is About and How It Came to Be

MUCH TO THE CONSTERNATION OF my loving wife, who thought she was marrying a stable tax attorney, I left my well-paying job to pursue my dream of starting a software company. While I was filled with unbridled optimism and confidence, looking back now it is safe to say that I was essentially clueless as to the ins and outs of establishing and running a small business. In fact, if I would have clearly understood the risks, I probably never would have made this leap, and I would be a partner at a Big Four accounting firm.

As they say, however, ignorance is bliss, and off I went. Developing the software was hard work, and instead of taking one year, it took three years to complete the "project," as my disappointed in-laws referred to it. Eventually, though, the product was ready to be introduced to the business community. I had the misguided impression that if the product was well designed and served a marketplace need, it would automatically find an audience and subsequently my fortunes would be made. Nothing could have been further from the truth.

Initially, figuring out how to get this new product into the hands of the customer was a struggle. I spent a good deal of time trying to learn from a wide variety of so-called "experts." The universal advice I

received was to read the best-selling book *Crossing the Chasm* by Geoffrey A. Moore.[1] This book was known as the sales and marketing bible
for high-tech companies because it laid out a well-defined strategy
on how to launch and conquer a marketplace. While the espoused
approach worked well at first, it quickly became apparent that this
tried-and-true methodology was not a panacea. Instead, this traditional way of selling dramatically increased the likelihood that my
nascent venture was going to struggle to survive.

Since failure was too painful to contemplate (it meant that my wife
and I would be living in my parents' guest bedroom), my management team and I gambled and pursued what was then a radical new
sales strategy. Instead of using an old-fashioned, direct sales force,
we began to use web-meeting software as a way to interact with our
prospects and clients. At first, we used this new technology simply to
qualify leads before our sales professionals went on the road for face-
to-face visits. However, it quickly became clear that prospects were
willing to license our product without the in-person visit. As a result,
our entire sales and support process centered around web meetings.
Over time, we developed an end-to-end sales assembly line based on
this technology, which hyperscaled our sales operation.

. This sales approach allowed a non-venture-capital-backed, thinly
capitalized company to market a mid-priced product profitably to the
business community on a national and international scale. Based on
this sales assembly line methodology, the company was propelled
from a small, struggling start-up into one of the largest tax software
companies in the world. Along the way, the sales approach gained a
life of its own and became known as an innovative way to sell technology to the business community.

When we decided to sell the company, a number of private equity
firms and leading enterprise software companies participated in the
bidding process in a competitive auction. While our products were

1   Geoffrey A. Moore, *Crossing the Chasm* (New York: HarperCollins, 1991).

certainly successful, the auction gained traction due to our web-meeting sales assembly line approach. Potential buyers believed that this sales platform could be used with other products and markets. For numerous reasons, Thomson Reuters had the winning bid, and the company was sold for $80 million.

Since that transaction, more and more companies have begun to employ high-velocity sales assembly lines in an attempt to conquer technology markets. That being said, I have worked with countless companies that understand this approach is a superior way (perhaps the *only* way) to successfully sell a technology product to the business-to-business (B2B) community, but they do not know how to implement the methodology efficiently, effectively, and in a manner that ensures its success. Instead, for the most part, companies have simply supplanted or even replaced in-person meetings with web meetings, broken off the sales development function from the account executives, and hoped for the best. Unfortunately, without also reimagining the underlying sales process, this change will not have the desired impact and often harms the seller.

This book is an introduction on how to use sales assembly lines to hyperscale your sales operation. Everything I have learned from working with my own start-ups, from other companies, and even from other experts on this exciting methodology is in this book. I had one goal in writing this, and that was for you to understand how critically important it is for your company to quickly conquer the mass market, and that a sales assembly line approach is the only strategy that will allow a company to not only thrive but survive. If this changes how you fundamentally think about sales to the business community, I have done my job.

I have also tried to include on every page at least one idea that will make a substantial difference in the day-to-day operations of your company's sales operation. In many ways, it is the guide I wished I had when I started my first company and was struggling to figure out how to establish a sales operation that would help my company scale and become the market leader. Whether you are a CEO, CFO, VP-Sales, or even a sales executive, you now have a resource at your disposal that will help you dramatically improve your sales volume.

Thank you so much for buying this book. If you have any questions or comments, please don't hesitate to get in touch with me at donald@assemblysales.com.

Why Is It So Hard to Sell B2B Technology Successfully?

WHEN I FOUNDED CROSSBORDER SOLUTIONS, the business press was regularly reporting on entrepreneurs who had made their fortunes by creating companies out of nothing but a good idea and some hard work. Based on my past work experience and knowledge of the market, I believed I had the key ingredients to create the next great company. So off I went into the great start-up unknown.

This type of unbridled optimism is the driving force behind every new company and product launch. While success stories abound, the glint of the gold at the end of the fabled rainbow hides the unpleasant truth that a majority of new companies fail. To comprehend the risk of starting a new venture, consider the fact that if a venture capital firm makes an investment in ten companies, on average, only two will become home runs, approximately five will fail outright, and the rest will struggle along, never realizing the initial goals of the founders or the investors behind the venture. What makes this statistic so sobering is that enterprises that receive institutional funding are among the best of the start-up community. The "experts" have designed a grueling winnowing process that is meant to "separate the wheat from the chaff." The fact that so many of these carefully vetted companies continue to come up short drives home the point that the fabled "rags to riches" story remains, to most people, simply a fairy tale.

If you were to ask a layperson for an explanation of why so many companies with a good product and a fertile market seem to struggle, most would hypothesize that an inability to get the product to market or the fact that market demand did not live up to initial expectations would be the reason. Unfortunately, this tends not to be the case. Let's look at the venture capital–backed company as an example. Companies that have raised institutional money have had their market analysis carefully scrutinized, and it is unlikely that everyone involved in the funding decision horribly misread the market potential. Furthermore, by the time professional money is involved, it is highly likely the first version of the product has been completed and the company has closed enough business to prove to the investors that the underlying concept is relatively sound.

Instead, I contend that many B2B technology ventures do not live up to expectations due to the fact that they are losers in a start-up game of survivor called the Gorilla Game. In this contest, early-stage companies compete to become the undisputed market leader, better known as the Marketplace Gorilla. The seller that moves the most product in the shortest amount of time wins! In any technology market, this is a winner-take-all competition, with the eventual market leader garnering more than 50 percent of the revenue and 75 percent of the profits from the space. While one or two other sellers might survive and even prosper, the invisible hand of the market will ensure that most of the other market participants struggle to survive or even fail entirely. Typically, this occurs because their sales method does not allow them to hyperscale their sales operation so that the company can reach and close enough companies in the mass market to succeed.

My first start-up software company, CrossBorder Solutions, found itself in this unfortunate losing position. Our product was originally priced at $25,000 annually so it would be attractive to middle-market companies. However, management quickly realized that at this low price point, the company would not be able to transform itself into a profitable, money-making venture if it relied on a direct sales force. Moreover, even if the price of its offering was raised dramatically and each transaction became profitable, the company still did not have access to the massive funds necessary to develop a direct sales force large enough to win over the mass market.

The company decided to make the most out of this crisis and use it as an opportunity to try and develop a new approach to B2B sales. To this end, we ignored the advice provided by the so-called experts and began to explore how web-meeting software could be used to distribute products and services to the business community in a more cost-efficient manner.

Using web-meeting software meant that sales professionals could conduct appointments in cyberspace rather than meeting in person with the prospect. Eventually, based on this technology, the company developed an end-to-end process that resembled a traditional manufacturing assembly line except that it was used to mass-produce sales. This sales assembly line methodology, which is the focus of this book, allowed the company to reach heights previously unimaginable for a company without VC funding. For example, consider the following:

- **Demo Performance.** Before adopting and implementing our web-meeting sales assembly line, our team of four sales professionals conducted three hundred product demonstrations per year, most of which were done at the prospects' work sites. At least a quarter of the meetings were second and third appointments. In the year that CrossBorder was sold, our team of eight sales professionals conducted thousands of demonstrations to potential clients in the United States and Europe.

- **Close Rate.** When the company's primary product was licensed using a direct sales approach, the company experienced a close rate of 10 percent (ratio of demos performed to demos converted to sales), which is considered a reasonable close rate when selling face-to-face. Once the sales assembly line methodology was fine-tuned, our sales team was able to achieve an across-the-board 18 percent close rate across multiple product lines.

- **Cost of Sales.** When we employed a direct sales force, each sale cost approximately $7,000. It is important to note that this number did not include any funds spent marketing the product. If these expenses were factored into the equation, the number would have been closer to $20,000 per sale achieved. With the new sales approach, we were able to bring this cost down to under $1,000 per customer.

- **Price Achieved.** When selling direct, the company's average deal price for its primary product was $22,000 annually. However, when employing the sales assembly line methodology, we were able to raise this price point to an average contract value of $75,000.

- **Client Breakdown.** With the web-meeting sales assembly line methodology, the company did not focus on any specific market segment. Moreover, the company did not derive substantial revenue from any one client or industry grouping. When the company was sold, it had more than two thousand distinct corporate customers. Moreover, while we were proud of our success with three hundred of the Fortune 1000 companies, we were equally enthused about our success with small and midsize enterprises (SME) contained in the Long Tail of the market (at sale, 77 percent of our clients had sales between $100 million and $500 million).

- **Growth Rate.** Since the sales assembly line approach was a high-volume methodology, CrossBorder Solutions was a high-growth company. From the year we started using the methodology until the year the company was sold, we enjoyed an average growth rate of 40 percent per year.

- **Financial Performance.** CrossBorder Solutions was a high-growth company that never raised significant outside capital but instead funded growth organically. In the first year the web-meeting sales assembly line methodology was adopted, the company realized approximately $3 million in revenue. When the company was sold three years later, it was forecasted to sell $30 million. Even more impressive than these revenue numbers were the operating margins we achieved. Due to the low cost associated with the sales model, the company enjoyed margins of greater than 50 percent on our mature product lines.

HOW DO WEB-MEETING SALES PEOPLE
SPEND THEIR WORKDAY

The average Web-Meeting logs more than 2,000 hours annually on emails, meetings, calls and more. **Here's how it breaks down:**

15% Administration

85% New Sales

34 HOURS PER WEEK NEW SALES

1700 HOURS PER YEAR NEW SALES

Due to its selling prowess, in spite of competing against better funded, more established competitors, CrossBorder Solutions became the market leader, or Marketplace Gorilla, in every product category it entered. When it became time to sell the company in an auction process, the driving force behind the transaction was its sales assembly line. The various strategic and private equity bidders believed the platform could easily be extended to their existing products and services. After a lengthy bidding process, CrossBorder Solutions became part of Thomson Reuters. In a nod to the importance of the sales assembly line approach, the press release announcing the terms of the sale stated that one of the main drivers behind the acquisition was CrossBorder Solutions' "innovative and powerful web-based sales approach" that the new owner hoped to adopt throughout its entire organization.

TIME SPENT SELLING
PER WEEK

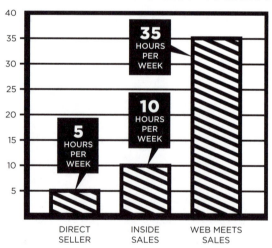

Since CrossBorder Solutions was sold, the use of web-meeting software in the technology sales arena has blossomed. Concurrently, sellers are regularly using the technology as a foundation when trying to implement high-velocity sales approaches designed to lower the cost of sales and increase sales volume. However, while the general idea has gained acceptance, the lack of a detailed road map on how to accomplish this method successfully has been an impediment to wide-scale adoption. This book is designed to bridge this knowledge gap by introducing a methodology known as a sales assembly line approach, which is designed specifically to help sellers hyperscale their sales operation and become the market leader in the space where they operate.

The first chapter will explain why it is difficult, if not impossible, for most B2B sellers to launch a new technology product into the mass market successfully. Specifically, this chapter will explore why companies relying on either a direct or inside sales model will find it difficult, if not impossible, to scale their sales operation in a manner necessary to survive. The second chapter will introduce the sales assembly line methodology and will show how a seller can use this approach to compete for a leadership position in the mass market. The third and fourth chapters will examine in detail how this sales approach can help supercharge the seller's performance by dramatically improving the close rate of the operation so the company is in the position to dominate the market and become the Marketplace Gorilla. Chapters five and six will explore the core principles of a sales assembly line, along with some helpful hints on how to optimize its operation.

Before embarking on this journey, an important point must be made clear. When outlining the sales methodology, the discussion is framed around how an early-stage technology company can employ this incredibly powerful sales approach. As a result, the reader might assume this methodology will work only within this limited fact pattern. *This is not the case!* In fact, the web-meeting sales assembly line approach espoused herein is a far superior method of selling to the business community than the direct or inside sales method, whether it be by a start-up or a large, established seller. To use this approach successfully, the seller needs to satisfy only two criteria. First, the seller must be able to demonstrate its product's value proposition using an online presentation format. For example, any firm that sells consulting services would fit this bill. Second, as this is a high-volume methodology, the target market size must be relatively large so the seller can fully benefit. If these two criteria are met, the methodology will allow the seller to quickly dominate a marketplace and become the market leader in a ridiculously profitable manner.

Without further delay, let's delve into this exciting sales approach!

CHAPTER 1

Launching a New B2B Technology Product or Service

1. STARTING THE JOURNEY

When determining how to launch a B2B software product and then conquer a marketplace, it is helpful first to gain an understanding of the contours of the market. Conventional wisdom holds that a bell curve, known as the Technology Adoption Life Cycle, is the best representation of a typical B2B technology marketspace. This curve is made up of five distinct segments, and each portion corresponds to a potential group of users of the new product, each of which has very different needs and buying characteristics. Visualized from left to right, as a product gains acceptance in the market, each segment becomes the potential group of customers that should be targeted next by the seller.

In his best-selling book *Crossing the Chasm*, Geoffrey A. Moore describes each buying segment. Specifically, on the far left of the curve are the Innovators. Innovators are "techies"—users who love new products simply because they are new. While they do not normally have the power within an organization to purchase the new technology, their opinions are respected by the rest of the organization, and they often serve as important gatekeepers to the rest of the organization.

In the next segment are the Early Adopters. Early Adopters are visionaries. Not only do they like new products because they are new, but they have the ability to envision how these products can be used to further their business goals. Moreover, they like to be on the forefront of change and are willing to implement innovative technologies, as they believe these tools give them a leg up over their competitors. To this end, they are comfortable working with new products and accept the problems that typically accompany any new product launch. These customers will likely be the start-up's first paying customers and early reference sites.

The Early Majority make up the next group of buyers. They are pragmatists who understand the power of technology and are willing to use new products if they clearly further the users' business goals. That being said, they are reluctant buyers of new, unproven technology, as they do not like taking unreasonable risks. As such, it is their preference to buy from the company that will likely become the market leader. It is critical that they be able to speak with happy references that can attest to the stability of the company and its product. Finally, as they are somewhat conservative, they need to buy a product that is relatively stable and includes most of the features necessary for a successful implementation.

Next on the continuum is the Late Majority. These are conservative buyers who are price sensitive, highly skeptical, and extremely demanding. They expect to receive a full product solution and will only buy the new product once the technology is firmly established in the Early Majority space and a clear market leader has been determined. Combined, these two segments make up the mass market for the product.

Last but not least, on the far right of the continuum are the laggards that do not believe in the power of the new solution. These companies are aware of the solution and the fact that their competitors are using it. In spite of this knowledge, they are willing to forgo its benefits. In sum, they do not like change and will never adopt the new solution, as they believe their "old way" of doing things will always be better. Technology companies will rarely be successful in marketing their solutions to these buyers.

With this understanding of the market, the seller of a B2B technology product must first figure out where the product stands on the bell curve. Knowing this location is an absolutely key factor because the sales approach that works at one stage of the continuum will likely not work in another. The needs and goals of both the buyer and the seller morph over time. The seller will continually need to evaluate and possibly change the sales approach to ensure it is constantly aligned with its goals as well as the goals of the buyers. While the method of interacting with the prospect might change, the chosen sales methodology must satisfy the following three criteria:

1. It must enable the seller to achieve a reasonable and sustainable profit (**Profit**).

2. It must be scalable, so it can successfully reach enough companies in the chosen market segment (**Volume**).

3. It must effectively convince prospective buyers to purchase the product or service at an appropriate and sustainable close rate (**Close Rate**).

CIRCLE OF SALES SUCCESS

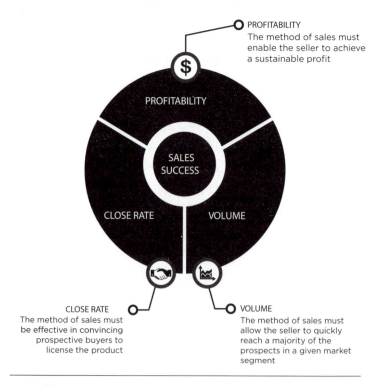

3 FACTORS OF SALES SUCCESS

PROFITABILITY
The method of sales must enable the seller to achieve a sustainable profit

PROFITABILITY

$

SALES
SUCCESS

CLOSE RATE

VOLUME

CLOSE RATE
The method of sales must be effective in convincing prospective buyers to license the product

VOLUME
The method of sales must allow the seller to quickly reach a majority of the prospects in a given market segment

For a technology company to achieve success in any given market segment, the seller's sales approach must satisfy all three of the above criteria!

For a company to achieve success in any given segment, the seller's sales approach must satisfy all three of the above criteria! If not, a company's prospects of success in the given market segment will be significantly diminished, and its growth trajectory will likely stall.

2. ATTACKING THE EARLY ADOPTER SEGMENT WITH A DIRECT SALES FORCE

Businesses have contemplated a number of different sales mechanisms since the industrial revolution. At the beginning of the twentieth century, enterprises relied on loose networks of sales agents distributed throughout the marketplace. However, in the 1950s, with the advent of a more robust transportation infrastructure, companies were in the position to rethink the structure of their sales operations. The result was the modern direct sales force that has been functioning without significant change for the past seventy years.

The defining characteristic of the direct sales force, regardless of the product being sold, is its absolute reliance on the concept that the individual sales professional would visit the prospect at his or her workplace to make the sale. This in-person approach allows the salesperson to develop a tight relationship with the buyer that presumably provides the prospect with the necessary comfort to move forward with the solution being offered. To ensure this occurs, it is not unusual for the salesperson to meet with the prospect multiple times. Due to the time spent on this effort, the average direct sales professional will meet, on average, with approximately eight new prospects per month and engage in five follow-up visits with prospects during the same period. Of course, if the salesperson is also responsible for post-sales support, the above new sales metrics can be substantially lower.

It is extremely expensive in terms of time and money to operate a direct sales force. To increase the efficiency and cost-effectiveness of the approach, almost all companies break up their marketplace into separate and distinct geographic territories. Under this scheme, depending on the size of the marketplace, one or more sales professionals are assigned to work with the prospects in a given territory. This is done to control travel costs and to increase the number of leads the salesperson can deal with cost effectively. In addition, since prospects often know one another within a tightly defined geographic area, territories should also help the seller build reference networks that should improve the prospect's comfort level with the salesperson and the solution being sold.

In the sales environment, the salesperson operating within a territory often acts in an independent fashion, "owning" the sales process from start to finish. Known as a Generalist, he or she is responsible for lead identification, direct marketing, cold-calling or appointment generation, and the actual sales process. To accomplish the job effectively, the professional is responsible for completely knowing the product and industry, inside and out. As if all that were not enough, in many cases the salesperson in the territory is also responsible for after-sale customer success, including upsell opportunities and renewals.

The following chart is a breakdown of the time a salesperson typically spends performing the above tasks. It is startling to note that under the Generalist model, a direct sales professional will spend only 12 percent of his or her time selling.[2]

Thus, spending only five hours per week, or 240 hours per year, dramatically impacts the sales throughput or new sales volume the sales professional can generate.

HOW DO DIRECT SALES PEOPLE
SPEND THEIR WORKDAY

The average direct sales professional logs more than 2,000 hours annually on emails, meetings, calls and more. **Here's how it breaks down:**

| 10% Lead Generation | 19% Customer Support/Sales | 16% Research |
| 12% New Sales | 15% Travel | 28% Administration |

5 HOURS PER WEEK NEW SALES   **240 HOURS PER YEAR** NEW SALES

---

2 Charles Fifield, "Necessary Condition #3—The Right Day-to-Day Operational Focus," *The Keller Center Quarterly Research Report* (January 2011).

This basic sales model is well supported by technology. In today's environment, almost all sales operations employ some sort of customer relationship management (CRM) software to manage their day-to-day sales operations. Based on the old-fashioned Rolodex, these database packages, such as Salesforce.com, were designed specifically to support and automate the activities of a direct sales force. Almost all of these tools are designed to help a Generalist effectively work prospects from start to finish in a defined territory. In addition, most are now cloud based so traveling sales professionals can have access to information from the road. Moreover, most packages assume the user will be handling relatively few leads, and as a result, the packages have not been optimized to support volume. The basic structure of these systems has certainly perpetuated the employment of the direct sales model.

Since this book is written from the perspective of a new product launch, I would like to introduce you to SocialFlow, a fictional company that is an amalgamation of start-up enterprises I have consulted with to jump-start B2B sales. This example, described in the following fact pattern, will be used throughout the book to evaluate different sales methodologies against the three criteria listed previously—Profit, Volume, and Close Rate—at each stage of the Technology Adoption Life Cycle.

SOCIALFLOW, A START-UP SOFTWARE COMPANY, FINISHED developing its first software product, which helped companies build online loyalty programs. Initially, the two founders served as the company's sales team. They were able to license the software to a handful of visionaries who were willing to try it. Once the product stabilized, the company hired two experienced sales professionals to work with the founders and attack the Early Adopter market. The goal at this stage of SocialFlow was to license the product to a handful of well-known companies that would be willing to serve as super references for the product.

The company's fledgling sales operation was relatively unsophisticated. Headquartered in New York City, the company divided the country into four territories, with a founder or salesperson assigned to each region. At first, they relied on personal industry contacts to generate leads. However, to supplement these leads, each professional was also responsible for identifying potential companies within his or her territory by cold-calling prospects. Once "live" leads, defined as prospects that wanted a demonstration of the software, were identified, an in-person visit occurred. To control the sales process, the company used Salesforce.com, the industry-leading, cloud-based CRM system developed in the early 2000s.

SocialFlow discovered that selling to Early Adopters was not an easy task. Plenty went wrong as they attempted to introduce buyers to the new solution. Although improvements were made, theirs was a minimally viable product and as such was still relatively immature and needed substantial work to meet the full-blown needs of the marketplace. Making this process even harder was the fact that the new sales team was figuring out, through a trial-and-error process, the product's market fit. It was still unclear what would drive potential buyers to license the product. In spite of these difficulties, the company was relatively successful in making inroads with Early Adopters. To this end, it secured a handful of clients that were willing to serve as enthusiastic references for the software solution.

Using the three criteria for a successful sales operation listed earlier, let's examine why the direct sales approach was the ideal method of sales when selling to the Early Adopter segment of the marketplace.

Profitability

At the early stages of a product launch, the importance of profitability is greatly reduced. It is quite acceptable and even expected that a young company should and will absorb losses while it sells a new product to Early Adopters. In this light, capital is normally set aside to cover the initial shortfall. Providing further leeway to the seller is the fact that, during this stage, the costs of sales are often greatly reduced. The seller is likely dealing with a relatively small number of parties that have either self-identified or have been found through personal connections with the seller. As a result, it is not necessary for the seller to embark on expensive marketing campaigns or to build out a large sales force.

Volume

The Early Adopter segment consists of approximately 10 percent of the buyers in any given market. Given its small size, a direct sales force can be effective in reaching and attacking these defined targets successfully. Moreover, as a practical matter, Early Adopter clients are often identified through personal industry contacts. The segment is also a safe choice, as many early-stage companies have within their grasp the ability, effort, and expense necessary to build an appropriately sized sales operation.

Close Rate

In general, Early Adopters like personal, one-to-one connections that are provided by face-to-face meetings with a company representative. This type of interaction enables the seller to build a powerful connection with the buyer that goes well beyond the traditional seller-customer relationship. This approach should allow these customers to self-identify with the seller and provide them with the emotional comfort necessary to move forward with the solution and to become powerful super references for the new product. Since the

Early Adopters are often seeking out the new solution, the close rate with these buyers is often relatively high.

Once success has been achieved with the Early Adopters (with success being defined as obtaining customers willing to serve as references), the seller will be in the position to attack the Early Majority portion of the mass market. At this point, the key to launching a successful product is to make a successful transition from the Early Adopters to this new group of buyers without stumbling.

3. TRANSITIONING INTO THE EARLY MAJORITY SEGMENT OF THE MASS MARKET

If selling to Early Adopters is like scaling Mount Everest, successfully introducing a product to the Early Majority segment is the equivalent of summiting K2. As we have discussed, Early Majority buyers are a difficult bunch of folks. They are pragmatists who are not interested in unfinished solutions. Instead, they are only looking to license a "complete" product that will do exactly what they need it to do and what the seller *says* it can do. The latter is extremely important, as the Early Majority has absolutely no interest in "making do" until the "next version" of the product is released. They want and need it to work immediately as advertised.

Making matters worse, if possible, is that pragmatist buyers are normally reluctant to deal with an early-stage company because they do not have the faith that such a company will survive over the long term. Instead, they feel more comfortable sticking with their current solution that comes from a more established vendor that has "stood the test of time" and can provide the necessary level of support and stability. This does not mean they are not interested in a new solution that can help propel their business forward, but only that they are content to gaze at the solution from afar and wait until they are sure that it is truly ready for "prime time."

As a consequence, it makes sense that the buyers in this segment of the market will only want to buy from the market leader or the company they perceive will be the market leader at some point in the near future. What often happens is that, at some point in the product adoption life cycle, pragmatists will begin to coalesce around one vendor, and this support will drive that company to become the market leader. Unlike in other industries, where multiple companies can share the limelight, in the technology space, it is a well-established truism that there can only be one market winner. This company is known as the Marketplace Gorilla. Normally, this is the first company to garner a 30 percent to 40 percent market share.

As Geoffrey Moore described in *Crossing the Chasm*, typically the "losers" in the market leadership battle are relegated to supporting roles. Specifically, the vendor who is in second or third place will become what is known as a *chimpanzee*. Chimpanzees are reasonable alternatives to the gorillas, who are often considered by pragmatist buyers, but they are picked at a much lower close rate. However, they make enough sales to survive and even prosper. At the bottom of the barrel are the monkeys. These are companies that become low-cost providers that service distinct niches of the marketplace. Since the gorilla and the chimpanzee continually encroach on the monkey's sphere of influence, monkeys are constantly beating back attacks that encroach on their rapidly dwindling sphere of influence and as such are in a constant struggle to survive. Unfortunately, the other market participants eventually fail entirely. See Appendix A for a full discussion on the history of gorillas in the marketplace.

The mass market, comprising the Early and Late Majority, is where most of the buyers of the potential solution reside. This is where most of the money from the technology product will be generated, which means there is no tomorrow for companies trying to succeed in this segment of the market. Specifically, in regard to revenue, Geoffrey Moore postulated that the gorilla will obtain approximately 50 percent of the revenue and 75 percent of the profits from any given market.

Thus, it is imperative that the seller of the new solution becomes the gorilla because this party gets all the bananas!

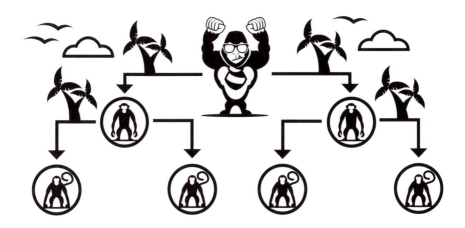

With a shift into this new buying segment, the seller now needs to develop a sales strategy that will meet the unique needs of the Early Majority. The first question that must be answered is whether the direct sales force remains an effective mechanism to sell to this new class of prospects.

4. INTRODUCTION TO THE GORILLA GAME

Moving into the Early Majority of the mass market is an exciting time for everyone involved in the product launch. As the offering has gained some degree of market acceptance, management's vision has finally been validated. The new enterprise is likely in the position to raise its first institutional round of financing. In addition to funding continued development efforts, often a large portion of these funds will be used to build out the sales and customer support staff. The

UNDERSTANDING THE
B2B SOFTWARE MARKET

MARKET CONTOURS

1 The Technology Adoption Life Cycle represents the various stages of the software market. Each segment corresponds to a different group of buyers. At each stage of the market, a B2B seller must determine what sales approach it will use to conquer that market segment.

2 Combined, the Early Majority and Late Majority make up the mass market where 80% of the revenue will be made, it is critical that the Seller successfully transition from the Early Adopters to the Early Majority.

MARKETPLACE GORILLA

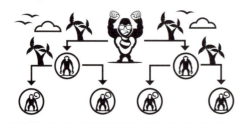

3 In a technology market, only ONE seller, called the Marketplace Gorilla can become the market leader. This seller will amass 50% of the revenue and 75% of the entire markets profits. Most other sellers, except for the 2nd place company, called the chimpanzee, will struggle to survive and will likely fail.

THE CHASM BETWEEN THE EARLY ADOPTERS AND EARLY MAJORITY

4 Unfortunately, the transition from the Early Adopter segment to the Mass Market is not a smooth one. Instead, a chasm between the two segments exists and a majority of companies will fall into this gap and fail.

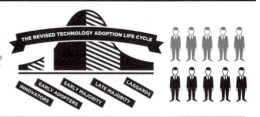

5 Whether a start-up lives or dies is largely dependent on whether the sales methodology that they chose to use to make the transition is appropriate. To be successful, the Sales Methodology must be comprised of the following:

 1) Must allow the seller to be profitable

 2) Must allow the seller to reach a significant portion of the mass market

 3) Must allow the seller to achieve a sustainable close rate.

company then seeks expanded office space to house the hordes of new employees that will soon be hired. Of course, this is all done in anticipation of the coming explosion in growth that occurs when a company transitions into the mass market.

All too often, though, this happiness is relatively short lived. Just when the company's growth should be exploding, the wheels start to fall off the bus. For the first time, forecasts begin to be missed. Instead of posting impressive growth numbers, sales begin to decline precipitously. Tense meetings are held with the new investors who are now, rightly so, concerned about their investment. Secret plans are being drawn up to replace the founders with "experienced" management who the investors hope will arrest the decline in time to save what was destined to be the "Next Great Thing."

The venture capital community has seen this process play out over and over again in early-stage companies. On average, if an institutional investor makes ten investments, at best, only two will become home runs—companies that are able to enter and conquer the mass market. Out of the remaining eight, a few will become "singles" or "doubles," which are investments that do not necessarily lose money but that do not make money, either. Usually these "successful" companies are likely to be permanently unprofitable and will only survive with continued infusions of capital from institutional investors until they are sold at a substantial discount. The rest of the investments, approximately five or six of them, will be outright failures and will not generate a minimally acceptable return on investment for the institutional investor.[3]

Unfortunately, this happens so frequently that it has become relatively commonplace; the situation is simply written off without much

---

3 Lending credence to this claim was a survey conducted by Mattermark. Their research showed that approximately 70% of recipients of seed rounds did not go on to raise a Series A round. It was shown that "from there on, the number of start-ups that raise a Series B round halves and continues to halve in a stepwise function through Series F and beyond." "The Start-up Funding Graduation Rate is Surprisingly Low," Jason Rowley, Mattermark.com, September 28, 2016.

thought. If pressed for a reason, most would blame either an unforeseen problem with the product, the product-market fit, or even the inexperience of the management team. However, this may not be the case. Instead, often this situation was preordained the moment the company's management naively decided to use the direct sales methodology employed so successfully with Early Adopters when selling to the Early Majority.

While selling to the Early Adopters was long believed to be the hardest stage of the product adoption life cycle, this notion is not accurate. The march up the slope of the technology adoption curve is not smooth and inviting. A seller cannot simply skip through the daffodils and sunshine, easily vanquishing all of its competitors and conquering the Early Majority with a snap of its fingers. Instead, the cruel, invisible handle of the technology marketplace ensures that the journey is through a dark, unforgiving place where only the strongest will survive. Remember, this winnowing process will allow only *one* company to come through relatively unscathed and emerge as the Marketplace Gorilla.

It is helpful to think of the technology adoption curve in a different light. Instead of a smooth transition between the Early Adopters and Early Majority buyers, it is well established that a gap exists between the two segments. In *Crossing the Chasm*, Moore postulated that this "chasm" exists due to a lack of suitable references and market discipline when using a direct sales force. This is not always so.

Instead, to understand this discontinuous path, imagine a very different landscape. It helps to think of the Technology Adoption Life Cycle as a game of "Start-up Survivor" called the Gorilla Game. Contestants with a new product start off on a desert island known as Great Expectations. In this windswept, barren place, sellers compete with one another to sell their new products to Early Adopters, using a direct sales force. Sellers who are unsuccessful at this task eventually starve and die.

The Gorilla Game re-imagines the Technology Adoption Life Cycle as a game of start-up survivor.

STAGE 1 — THE ISLAND OF GREAT EXPECTATIONS

Secure Early Adopter References: Contestants with a new technology product start off on a desert island known as the Island of Great Expectations. At this stage, the seller must compete with other companies to sell to Early Adopters. Companies that land enough customers to serve as references are able to move on to the next stage of the competition. Those that are unsuccessful starve and die off.

Transition to the Mass Market: To get off the Island of Great Expectations, companies must build a bridge to the Mainland where the mass market resides. Each bridge is comprised of the Seller's sales approach that will be used to attack the Early Majority segment. The key to surviving this stage is to build a stable bridge that is supported by three pillars, each of which corresponds to the three criteria of a successful sales organization. If the chosen approach is incorrect, the bridge will collapse and the seller will fall into the sea, unlikely to survive.

STAGE 2 — BUILDING A BRIDGE

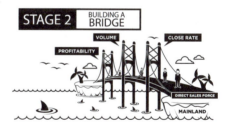

STAGE 3 — CONQUERING MASS MARKET

Compete to Become Marketplace Gorilla: In the third and final stage of the competition, if the Seller constructed a stable bridge, it can crossover to the Mainland. Here, the remaining sellers will compete against each other in a death match over the Mass Market. The seller that moves the most product in the shortest amount of time wins and is anointed the market leader or the Marketplace Gorilla!

Companies that land enough customers willing to serve as references move on to the second stage of the competition. To get off the island, each survivor needs to build a bridge to the lush, tropical mainland where the mass market resides. Each bridge will be formed by the company's sales approach that will be used to attack the Early Majority segment. The key to success at this stage of the competition is to build a stable bridge supported by three pillars, each of which corresponds to one of the three criteria of a viable sales organization. But if the chosen approach is incorrect, then the bridge will collapse and the sellers will find themselves in the sea, struggling to survive.

If the chosen sales methodology works, the seller can cross into the mass market. This is where the third and final stage of the competition occurs. Here, the companies that have been successful in the first two stages compete directly against one another in a knock-down, drag-out death match. The company that sells the most product in the shortest amount of time wins and is anointed the Marketplace Gorilla. The losers of the Gorilla Game either fail entirely or are relegated to being one of the other types of primates that might survive but never meet the market's initial expectations.

With an understanding of the rules of the Gorilla Game, let's start off by examining whether a company can use the direct sales force that was so successful with Early Adopters as a bridge to the Early Majority.

Pillar One: Can the Direct Seller Achieve Profitability?

When a software product is first introduced to the Early Adopters, profitability can and often does take a backseat to the effort of simply getting the software into the customer's hands. However, once the seller enters the Early Majority, the seller can no longer adopt such a laissez-faire attitude. In fact, it becomes absolutely critical that the seller begin to generate profits in this section of the bell curve.

A company that is selling an expensive product can certainly achieve profitability using a direct sales force. However, what about the majority of sellers that would like or need to sell a product priced below $150,000 *annually*? Unfortunately, for these sellers, profitability will be difficult to achieve if they employ a direct sales force. To illustrate this point, let's return to SocialFlow, our B2B seller of loyalty software.

SOCIALFLOW SUCCESSFULLY LICENSED ITS PRODUCT TO A handful of Early Adopters, and it was able to make the move into the Early Majority segment. To this end, significant outside capital was raised from a leading institutional investor. The raised funds were primarily used for marketing purposes and to build out the initial sales force. The company chose to continue to employ a direct sales approach, since it was working so well with the Early Adopters, and to license its product using a Software as a Service (SaaS) model under which the product was licensed for $50,000 annually.

The company targeted small to midsize enterprises, as a slew of other companies were already selling loyalty software to large-cap companies. After conducting marketing studies, the company believed the available market was 75,000 prospects in the United States. There were rumors that one or more other start-ups were planning to launch a similarly positioned product. Therefore, everyone was concerned the company's first go-to-market advantage might be at risk.

These were the core assumptions associated with Social-Flow's direct sales model:

Number of Sales Professionals	4
Base Salary of Sales Professionals	$80,000
Commission Rate	12% of gross sales

Number of Sales Engineers	1
Base Salary of Sales Engineer	$80,000 annually
VP-Sales	$300,000 annually
Salary Overhead	50%
Close Rate	10%
Price of Product	$50,000 annually
No. of First Appointments	8 per salesperson per month
No. of Follow-up Appointments	4 per salesperson per month
Average Direct Costs of an Appointment	$4,000
Direct Sales Costs	$300,000
Renewal Rate	80%

IMPORTANT CAVEATS

- The above costs *did not* include the other costs of running the company. For model purposes, assume that sales and marketing expenses made up 30 percent of the overall burn of the company due to the ongoing software development costs.

- The sales engineer traveled to half of the follow-up appointments with the sales professional. The VP-Sales traveled to 25 percent of the follow-up appointments. Neither of these two professionals traveled to any first appointments.

- Sales professionals functioned as Generalists and were responsible for prospecting and setting up their own appointments, making the sales, as well as preparing correspondence, proposals, and purchase orders. In addition, the sales professionals were responsible for providing assistance to customers, including obtaining renewals.

- Each salesperson was paid the same commission for renewal sales as for new sales.

When the above assumptions are taken into account, management was pleased to discover that at a $50,000 price point
and a 10 percent close rate, the company achieved $1.5 million
in annual sales. However, this seemingly impressive number was
tempered by the fact that the direct expense associated with
the sales effort amounted to approximately $3.8 million. While
this $2.3 million loss is clearly distressing, everyone was beside
themselves with grief when the realization hit home that the
loss in actuality was going to be three times larger when non-
sales-related expenses were factored into the equation. There
was the fleeting hope that once renewals kicked in, this loss
would have been somewhat mitigated. This was not the case.
The loss on the *sales operation* continued until year four.

In fact, when selling a technology product, a company using a
direct sales force would need to charge more than $400,000 per client
to make money in its first year. If the company was content to wait
three years to reach profitability, it would need to charge $220,000
annually. Unfortunately, a company charging under $150,000 would
need to wait upward of ten years to make a profit. As such, in this
case, the profitability pillar holding up the bridge to the mainland has
crumbled, and the direct seller will fall to the bottom of the sea. This
result stems from a combination of the high costs of sales and the low
throughput of each sales professional.

Pillar Two: Can the Direct Seller Reach the Necessary Number of Buyers?

One of the fundamental premises of a technology marketspace, mentioned earlier, is that the business community will eventually coalesce
around one supplier. This means that a seller who is attempting to

secure the gorilla position must enter into a zero-sum game with the other market participants. In short, *the seller that moves the most product in the smallest amount of time wins.* Since the key to winning this battle is to gobble up market share, the seller must find a way to reach and sell to as many customers as possible at a dramatically quicker pace than the other market participants. Moreover, each year, as the pool of available prospects shrinks, this task becomes more and more difficult. The question then becomes, Can a seller employing a direct sales force accomplish this task in a quick enough time frame and for a reasonable expense? Unfortunately, as the next example demonstrates, in any sizable market, a direct seller will have a difficult time scaling its sales operation to the degree necessary to make a noticeable impact.

IN THE CASE OF SOCIALFLOW, EACH OF THE FOUR SALES professionals were meeting with eight new prospects per month. This rate meant that in the first year, the company's sales force would have met with 384 prospects, and assuming a 10 percent close rate, it would have closed a grand total of thirty-eight customers. With these sales numbers, in a market of over 75,000 prospects, SocialFlow clearly was not going to become the de facto market standard anytime soon. In fact, with this limited reach, the company likely was going to find itself relegated to the bottom of the proverbial barrel, especially if an established seller with a large sales force entered the middle market or one of the other start-up companies was able to reach and close more potential customers.

Luckily, SocialFlow, with its raised capital, was able to put aside any thoughts of short-term profitability. Instead, with this money in hand, the company's goal was to grow as fast as possible, gobble up market share, and hopefully become the

Marketplace Gorilla. To do so, the company decided to build out the biggest sales force possible to obtain a 40 percent market share in short order.

Under an aggressive three-year plan, the company estimated it would need to secure thousands of new clients per year to achieve this goal. Assuming the same 10 percent close rate and taking into account the standard 50 percent salesperson failure rate, the company needed to hire hundreds of sales professionals. Putting aside the enormous expense associated with this effort (three hundred sales professionals would cost over $200 million per year), it was almost an impossibility for the company to identify and onboard that many qualified sales professionals so quickly. As such, its client goal was clearly too aggressive.

Instead, the company was successful in onboarding twenty new professionals. Unfortunately, the team's expected close rate would likely drop from 10 percent to 8 percent due to the dilution of talent. If the average number of new appointments stayed the same, after these almost herculean efforts, the company would have only added approximately 150 new clients and still lost significant money on its sales operation in the first year!

The above demonstrates that the primary issue facing a direct seller is that the throughput of each sales professional is simply not high enough. Moreover, it is impossible, except for a few special cases, from a cost or resource perspective to solve this issue by powering through and simply increasing the number of overall professionals. Therefore, a seller using a direct sales force will find it difficult to reach enough prospects in the Early Majority market to become the Marketplace Gorilla. In this case, the second pillar of the direct sales bridge has collapsed as well.

Pillar Three: Can the Direct Seller Be Successful in Convincing Buyers to Purchase?

In our three-part evaluation, the final step is to determine whether a direct sales force continues to be an effective method to convince a prospect to purchase the goods or services under consideration. Remember, B2B sellers have been using this approach in one form or another for decades. Furthermore, many business buyers have been conditioned to expect and accept this method of selling. However, these facts do not necessarily mean that a direct sales force will provide the highest close rate. In fact, over the last decade, commentators have suggested that the direct sales force does not work as well as it should. For example, HubSpot recently released a survey that found 40 percent of sales forecasts are incorrect and that the turnover of sales professionals in most organizations averages 30 percent per year. That being said, a discussion of this magnitude is beyond the scope of this book, and so for these purposes let's assume that the direct sales force remains an effective mechanism to close deals successfully. In any event, it simply does not matter because the other two pillars of sales success have failed so spectacularly. Achieving a decent close rate is at best a conciliatory prize.

In sum, B2B sellers that rely on a direct sales force to sell product within the Early Majority market will find it difficult to achieve profitability or to assume a market leadership position. This demonstrates that although the direct sales force was a suitable method to identify Early Adopters, it does not work once the seller is attacking the Early Majority segment. The direct seller's bridge to the mass market will have collapsed, and the enterprise is apt to wind up floating in the sea, where it will likely drown.

BUILDING A STABLE BRIDGE

THE CONTESTANT

Seller Employing a Direct Sales Approach

SALES 1.0 GENERALIST MODEL

CORRESPONDENCE

TRAVEL   SALES

COLD CALLING   CLIENT SERVICES

MARKETING   UPSALES

LEAD IDENTIFICATION   RENEWALS

TIME SPENT SELLING

In a Direct Seller environment, the sales person operating within a territory owns the sales process from start to finish. Known as a Generalist, he or she will be responsible for every aspect of the sale from lead identification to customer success to renewals.

SALES APPROACH DETAILS

PROFITABLITY

The defining characteristic of the direct sales force is the absolute reliance on having the sales professional visit the prospect at his or her workplace to make the sale. This is very expensive.

FEBRUARY

SALES VOLUME

Due to the limited amount of time spent actually selling (10%), direct sellers can only do 8 new and 8 follow-up appointments per month.

CLOSE RATE

Selling face-to-face, a direct seller should enjoy a close rate of 8-12%.

THE RESULT: Will the Bridge Stand?	Formula for Sales Success		
	PROFITABILITY	VOLUME	CLOSE RATE
	✗	✗	✓

VOLUME   CLOSE RATE

PROFITABILITY

DIRECT SALES FORCE

MAINLAND

5. POSSIBLE LIFELINES TO THE
DROWNING COMPANY

If a B2B technology company's sales suddenly stall after some degree of initial success, there is a good chance that the seller chose the wrong sales approach and the bridge to the mass market has collapsed. While the company's position is certainly dire, all is not lost. The seller can still survive if it can find a way to keep its head above water and make its way back to the island of Great Expectations. Once on its barren shores, the seller can try a different crossing or sales approach. As the saying goes, money solves 99 percent of all problems. The best way for a seller to stay afloat is to increase its short-term revenue position. By manipulating the interplay between the volume of appointments with prospects, the close rate, and the price the product is licensed for, the seller will be in the position to drive immediate revenue growth and buy time to reevaluate its approach to attacking the mass market opportunity. This concept can be best expressed by the following mathematical formula:

$$\text{Close Rate} \times \text{Volume} \times \text{Price} = \text{Revenue}$$

Conventional wisdom holds that price has the greatest influence on revenue. However, this is not the case. All three factors in the above equation are equally important and carry the same weight. Moreover, it is critically important to understand that changing one factor will almost always have an impact on the other two. Care must be taken to ensure that any increase or decrease in one determinant of revenue will not result in the seller being put into an even worse position. With this in mind, a number of strategies can be considered.

Approach One: Improve the Close Rate

One option is to raise the all-important close rate, which is defined as the ratio of the number of deals closed to the number of appointments generated. The typical way to do this is to bring in more experienced sales professionals and even "mature" sales management who have worked in successful sales operations in the past, with the hope they can apply their "expert knowledge" to the situation at hand. While this approach can certainly make a positive impact, the end result normally is less than ideal.

While significantly raising the close rate is a good idea, it is easier said than done. Every product has a natural rate that corresponds to its method of sales and its position on the Technology Adoption Life Cycle bell curve. For the typical product being sold by a direct sales force to the Early Adopter market, a seller can expect to achieve a close rate of 6 percent to 8 percent. When dealing with the Early Majority, the average seller can expect a rate of 8 percent to 12 percent. As such, unless the seller makes a wholesale change to its sales approach, the best it can hope for is at most a couple of point upticks in the close rate. While a higher closing rate is a positive development, this alone will unlikely save the company. For example, with SocialFlow at the $50,000 price point, the loss, which was directly attributable to the sales operation, would continue until the close rate rose from 10 percent to 22 percent. For the entire company to reach profitability, it would have had to achieve a close rate of over 90 percent. In either case, this type of increase is unrealistic and impossible to achieve.

Approach Two: Increase Appointment Volume

Another approach is to have the sales professionals work with more leads and hence make more sales. While this is a reasonable approach, it is important to understand that once sales professionals are traveling to sales meetings, it is hard, if not impossible, to pursue a volume-based strategy. The general rule of thumb is that a direct sales professional who is a Generalist cannot do more than two *new* sales visits per week and still have time to handle his or her pipelines appropriately. Typically, once this number is exceeded, the sales professional's other responsibilities will begin to suffer. This will likely lower the all-important close rate, which then counteracts any moderate gains achieved by the small increase in volume.

For the moment, however, let's suspend this assumption and pretend that it is somehow possible for the direct sales professionals to handle a significantly greater number of prospects. Typically, in the direct sales environment, raising the number of appointments due to the costs of the sales operation has practically no positive impact on the overall revenue of the company. At SocialFlow, for example, if each sales professional were to conduct twenty new appointments and ten follow-up appointments, the company's direct sales operation would still lose more than $3.7 million, which is practically the same amount lost when each sales professional was doing eight new and four follow-up appointments in the base case. In fact, mathematically, no number can help SocialFlow out of its predicament as long as a direct sales force is employed.

Approach Three: Raise Product Price

For most companies, the most common approach to raising short-term revenue is to raise the price of the product being licensed. In fact, it is not usual for a start-up enterprise to calculate its burn and then set the price for the product based on the calculation of what is necessary to exceed the burn number or even a number to support its valuation. Raising the price is certainly one factor that can make an immediate and discernible difference in the fortunes of the seller. Unfortunately, raising the price of the product is not always a panacea, and it can be detrimental in certain cases.

Price cannot be determined in a vacuum. While many factors should be considered, the price's interplay with a product's close rate is of critical importance. At every possible price point, a product will have a natural close rate. As the price of a product rises, demand—and therefore the associated close rates—will fall. The question becomes, How far will it fall? On a percentage basis, if close rates fall more than the price rises, then the increase will have been for naught. Therefore, the seller needs to be careful when attempting a price increase and must attempt to discover a pricing equilibrium where the highest price intersects with the highest close rate possible.

In the case of SocialFlow, the company had achieved a 10 percent close rate at a $50,000 price point. At this price, in the first year, the company's sales operation was losing approximately $2 million. At $110,000, if the close rate remained the same, the sales operation would break even. However, if the close rate dropped even one point to 9 percent, the sales operation would once again be in a loss position.

Also important is that raising the price of the product will have a negative impact on the seller's volume of appointments. Specifically, as the price of a product rises, the market for B2B products can quickly become exponentially smaller. In the B2B community, the rule of thumb is that once a product is priced above $100,000 annually, a significant falloff in potential customers occurs. At this price point or higher, the market generally segments itself into a group of companies that have yearly annual sales of over $300 million. In the United States, one would think this is a big market. However, surprisingly, only a few thousand US publicly traded companies have sales in excess of $300 million.

This smaller number of potential customers can have a negative impact in two related ways. First, a seller will find it much more difficult to obtain the necessary volume of appointments to keep the sales staff busy, simply because there are fewer names to call. Second, it is much harder to reach prospects in larger companies. Moreover, in addition to the appointment-generation close rate being lower, the actual sales close rate will also drop once the seller begins to focus on larger enterprises. It is difficult and time consuming to sell big deals to very large companies. Therefore, when taken together, the decrease in close rate will often counteract any increase in price.

Approach Four: Change Deal Structure

Closely related to raising the price of the software is the strategy of changing the underlying structure of the licensing arrangement. Today, it is fashionable to use a subscription model when licensing software. While establishing a strong long-term renewal stream will help the company from a revenue standpoint down the road and will certainly help the seller immediately achieve a higher valuation in the short run, this model is not the seller's friend. Just when the new enterprise needs cold, hard cash the most, this licensing model helps to ensure that cash is not available. This is especially the case when one considers that the price a seller can achieve in a SaaS environment on an annual basis can be significantly less than what could be obtained if the software was licensed using a perpetual licensing scheme. One approach is to switch over from a subscription model to a perpetual licensing strategy. However, this change will result in an up-front price increase that can negatively impact the seller's volume and close rate. In addition, the company's valuation likely will fall, which can make raising outside capital more difficult.

Approach Five: Continued Subsidization of the Sales Force

Certainly, the most common survival approach is for a high tech company is to eschew profitability as well as market dominance and to raise more outside funds. While counterintuitive, due to the difficulties associated with building a profitable business that can secure a market leadership position, this has become the standard approach for venture capital–backed enterprises. While using outside funds to mask underlying problems with a business can help the business survive, it has significant downsides.

First and foremost, successive rounds of financing will result in equity dilution for the founders and initial investors. While the old adage of owning a small piece of a bigger company sounds good, this does not always work out as planned, especially when profitable sales are difficult to achieve. Second, upon an income-producing event, any valuation that the seller will receive will be significantly lowered by the fact that its sales operations remain unprofitable. In addition, the seller must also consider what happens if follow-on financing becomes unavailable due to difficult market conditions. Finally, institutional investors, founders, and employees should be aware that if the outside money cannot drive the company to become the Marketplace Gorilla, the company's valuation will eventually decline and the company will eventually fail.

6. BUILDING A NEW SALES BRIDGE

As we have shown, for most companies launching a new product, using a direct sales force to attack the mass market will likely stall any forward momentum. Instead of experiencing the explosive growth as expected, the seller is apt to begin a downward spiral. At this point, it is absolutely critical that the seller swims back to the island of Great Expectations and immediately arrests the decline. To this end, a number of strategies can provide the seller with some breathing room while it reevaluates its sales options.

However, the only true way to get back into the Gorilla Game and have the opportunity to compete in the mass market is to once again try and make a successful crossing. To do so, the company must attempt to construct a new sales bridge, which is based on a different sales methodology. This section explores two alternative pathways that B2B sellers often try to employ.

Approach One: Third-Party Distribution Arrangements

One alternative is to outsource the selling of the product to another company that has an established sales force. On its face, third-party distribution arrangements seem to solve the three issues vexing the direct seller. First, if structured correctly, the agreement should establish a reasonable profit margin for the developer of the product. Second, if the right distributor is chosen, this company should have the resources in place to be able to reach a large number of prospects successfully in the mass market. Finally, if the distributor has been successful in selling other products, there is a good chance that the sales force can achieve a sustainable close rate.

The danger with these types of deals is twofold. First, in the early stages of a product launch, it will be difficult, if not impossible, for the third party to provide any meaningful, concrete sales guarantees and therefore royalty payments to the developer. It is simply too hard to forecast how the new product will do in the mass market. As such, these arrangements will often turn into "Barney" relationships, where both parties hug and agree to love each other, but nothing ever really gets accomplished.

Second, even if the seller was able to obtain a minimum guarantee, the third-party seller could still struggle to make sales of the new product. This situation could occur for many reasons. For example, even if there is nothing wrong with the product or its market potential, the line sales force might simply decide not to push the new product, despite management's directive. In this case, while the developer will receive its minimum guaranteed royalty, it is unlikely that this amount will properly compensate the developer for its efforts. In addition, it will likely not propel the product being sold into a market leadership position. Once this occurs, it is typically game over for the developer, as the company has not developed an alternative sales channel, and it is often difficult to do so once the product has "failed" in the marketplace.

Therefore, while third-party distribution arrangements might be a reasonable approach to consider once the seller is firmly entrenched in the mass market and wants to pursue it as a complementary sales channel, it is simply too risky a proposition to use as a crossing mechanism between the Early Adopter and Early Majority segments.

Approach Two: Inside Sales

In the past three years, a new way to sell has begun to supplement or even replace the traditional direct sales approach. This alternative approach, which is known as inside sales or Sales 2.0, is a pure volume play that was designed to help companies dramatically improve the throughput or the number of prospects worked at any given time by a sales team. In theory, this increase not only assists sellers in reaching profitability but also in conquering the mass market. While there is no exact definition of this volume-enhancing approach, the following common characteristics are often present.

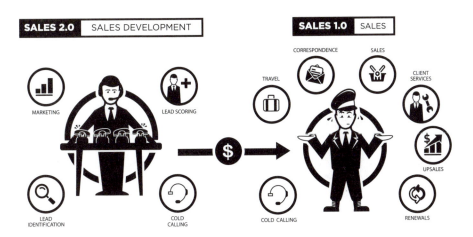

First and foremost, inside sales organizations partially or fully remove the lead-generation function from the sales professionals. This appointment-generation responsibility is given to telemarketers who are now known as sales development representatives (SDRs), who identify potential prospects in the marketplace and then cold-call or email them in an attempt to schedule qualified appointments called opportunities. Opportunities are passed on to the actual sales professionals, who close them in the normal course. Breaking off lead generation allows the sales professional to double the time spent selling, as compared to the direct sales Generalist. Specifically, the salespeople are now able to spend a whopping ten hours per week or five hundred hours per year selling!

HOW DO INSIDE SALES/SALES 2.0 SALES PEOPLE
SPEND THEIR WORKDAY

The average Inside Seller logs more than 2,000 hours annually on emails, meetings, calls and more. **Here's how it breaks down:**

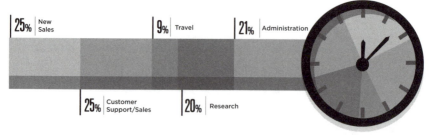

25% New Sales

9% Travel

21% Administration

25% Customer Support/Sales

20% Research

10 HOURS PER WEEK NEW SALES

500 HOURS PER YEAR NEW SALES

Second, inside sales organizations will likely use web-meeting software, such as WebEx or GoToMeeting, in some capacity to conduct online appointments with qualified opportunities. This is especially the case in regard to technology companies. For example, today, it is unusual to see a software company that does not have a button on their website that allows the user to click and sign up for a web-meeting demonstration.

Web-meeting software typically is used in one of two ways. First, especially for companies selling an expensive solution, web meetings are often used as a qualifying tool. The salesperson will generally give a short PowerPoint presentation and conduct an abbreviated presentation of the solution using the web-meeting technology. This approach allows the seller to give the potential buyers a 60,000-foot overview of the product and service and to determine whether the lead is actually "live." If it is, the lead is then worked in the normal course of a direct sales approach. Second, some sellers have completely eliminated their direct sales forces and replaced in-person meetings with web meetings. Under this scenario, the seller not only qualifies the prospect over the web but also attempts to close the buyer without ever meeting with the client face-to-face.

Third, understanding the limitations of traditional CRM solutions, inside sales companies often employ specialized software to improve the effectiveness of the sales development representatives and increase their throughput. These software packages often sit on top of the seller's CRM system and allow the seller to build a "sales stack." For example, Marketo allows sellers to score or rate prospects so sales development representatives have a better likelihood of achieving a successful sales call. Another example is InsideSales.com, which has developed software that helps sales development representatives increase their call volume dramatically by using artificial intelligence to determine the optimal prospect to call.

With this loose description of the inside sales approach, let's examine whether the methodology can meet the incredibly high expectations of the sales community and serve as a reasonable bridge from the Early Adopter segment to the mass market. Once again, to make this determination, it is necessary to understand how the approach stacks up against the three criteria of a successful sales methodology.

Pillar One: Can the Inside Sales Organization Achieve Profitability?

One of the principal factors behind an unprofitable sales force is the cost associated with in-person appointments. Therefore, an inside sales approach can increase the seller's profitability by reducing the costs of sales through the use of web-meeting software. In the SocialFlow example, if the seller employed the technology to qualify appointments and subsequently reduced travel by 50 percent, the company's loss on its sales operation would be reduced to $1.4 million. If travel was completely eliminated, the loss would be reduced to $270,000. While this is a step in the right direction, this change on its own is not large enough to drive the inside sales company to profitability.

The second way using inside sales can improve profitability is by increasing the throughput of the sales professional. By separating the cold-calling function from the actual selling process, the sales professional can roughly double his or her throughput. If all other factors are held equal, the inside sales organization should be able to realize a corresponding increase in sales revenue. Of course, if the costs of sales do not rise in conjunction with this increase, significant profitability gains will result. For example, if SocialFlow doubled the number of appointments, doubled its sales volume, and also lowered its costs by eliminating travel, the company's direct sales operation would become profitable to the tune of $1 million in the first year! Unfortunately, the seller as a whole would still lose over $4 million the first year and remain in a loss position until year five.

Simply breaking off the lead-generation function does not always result in the expected gains, for a number of reasons. In many organizations, even though the lead generation is broken off, many sellers do not properly optimize the cold-calling effort. It is not unusual to see the SDR making relatively few phone calls and therefore obtaining a limited number of qualified leads. Normally, this occurs because the SDR is spending time researching leads or finding the perfect name to call.

There are also problems on the sales side of the equation. While breaking off the lead-generation function is a step in the right direction, the salesperson is often still responsible for many non-sales-related tasks that can take up to 80 percent of his or her time. This is especially true if sales professionals are still traveling to the prospect, which greatly limits their overall throughput and therefore dramatically dampens the resulting improvement in profitability. Also, as most CRM packages were built with direct sellers in mind, the systems have not been optimized to handle volume. This can negatively impact their efficiency and effectiveness as well as lower the overall sales volume.

However, the biggest impediment to realizing any benefit accrued from breaking off the lead-generation function is the ingrained behavior patterns of the sales professionals themselves. Many sales professionals are so used to dealing with a relatively small number of leads that it becomes difficult, if not impossible, to transform them into true volume sellers. Often, if they get more leads from the sales development representatives, they simply cherry-pick the opportunities to find the best ones rather than work all of them to their fullest extent, which greatly limits the upside of the approach.

In sum, using a team of dedicated sales development professionals will certainly improve the financials of an inside sales organization. However, the increase in sales throughput is often not enough to change the overall equation. Specifically, in our above example, a 100 percent increase in sales volume and the elimination of travel through the use of web-meeting software will result in the seller having a profitable sales organization but will unfortunately still result in the seller realizing an overall loss. Therefore, an inside sales organization will find it difficult to satisfy the profitability criteria of a successful sales bridge to the mainstream market.

Pillar Two: Can an Inside Sales Seller Reach the Necessary Number of Buyers?

We have shown that a seller using a direct sales force has almost no hope of reaching enough prospects to become the market leader. By separating the sales development function from the actual sales process, however, the seller should be able to obtain more leads, more sales, and therefore a larger number of customers. The question becomes whether this increase is enough to help the inside seller achieve market dominance and win the Gorilla Game. In our Social-Flow example, an increase in sales volume of 100 percent will result in the company obtaining sixty-one new customers per year. Even with twenty sales professionals, the organization would only gain 307 customers. While this is certainly a dramatic improvement, the volume achieved is simply not enough to help the company conquer the mass market in a short enough time period to become the market leader.

Pillar Three: Can the Inside Sales Organization Achieve a Sustainable Close Rate?

In most situations, sellers using web meetings as part of their sales process have simply replaced their direct sales appointments with the new medium. The presentation and overall approach to dealing with the prospect have stayed the same, except that the seller does not meet with the prospect face-to-face. The impact of this approach can be and often is disastrous!

Unless a wide variety of steps are taken that take advantage of the unique features of the web-meeting sales environment, a web meeting *does not* in any way, shape, or form approximate an in-person appointment. In fact, if the web-meeting environment is not optimized appropriately, the close rate associated with this approach will often fall dramatically. A recent survey by InsideSales.com found that the close rate of sellers in the technology industry fell 4.7% in 2015.[4]

Because the close rate is such an important factor in helping the seller enter and succeed in the mass market, a failure in this area can leave the seller in a much worse position than it would have been if it kept using a direct sales approach. Remember, there is a one-to-one relationship between close rate, sales volume, and price. Therefore, a lower close rate can and often does erase any volume gains achieved by removing the cold-calling function from the sales professional. In the SocialFlow example, if the company eliminated the travel cost, increased throughput by 100 percent, but also experienced a 25 percent decline in the close rate, the company would still be operating at a substantial loss.

As with the third-party distribution option, the inside sales model certainly has some attractive benefits when compared to the standard direct sales approach. If perfectly optimized, this approach can moderately help the seller in each of the three principal areas of sales success. But in the real world this is unlikely to be the case, especially since a set of best practices has not been clearly developed, which greatly limits the methodology's effectiveness and can make its implementation extremely risky. Therefore, while inside sales companies have seen an improvement in overall sales results, it has not been the game changer that the start-up community had hoped for. After all, it is hard to get excited about a sales program that only promises a smaller loss. Adding credence to this unenthusiastic view of the inside sales methodology is the fact that although there has been a dramatic increase in the use of this approach, B2B companies

---

4   Business Growth Index, March 29, 2016, InsideSales.com.

are still failing at roughly the same alarming rate. If this were the panacea everyone from founders to investors had hoped for, this solution should have translated into a dramatic improvement in the fortunes of the B2B start-up community. This has not occurred.

THE CONTESTANT

Seller Employing an Inside Sales/Sales 2.0 Approach:

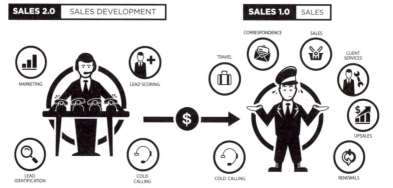

The defining characteristic of an Inside Seller is that the lead generation function is broken off from the sales professional and given to a specialized resource known as a Sales Development Representative. The sales person still retains significant responsibilities in making the sale and supporting the client.

22% TIME SPENT SELLING

SALES APPROACH DETAILS

PROFITABLITY

An Inside Seller will often use web-meeting software alone or in conjunction with on-site visits which lowers costs of sales and moderately improves profitability.

SALES VOLUME

By breaking off the lead generation function and limiting travel, the seller is able to significantly increase sales volume to 16 new appointments per month

CLOSE RATE

Due to the use of web-meeting software, the close rate is often lower than a direct sales professional.

THE RESULT: Will the Bridge Stand?	Formula for Sales Success		
	PROFITABILITY	VOLUME	CLOSE RATE
	—	✗	✗

7. CONCLUSION

When a company first launches a product, a direct sales force is a powerful tool to identify initial customers and build a reference base. While succeeding with the Early Adopter segment is important, if the seller is going to be successful, it needs to move from this relatively small segment into the mass market. The mass market is where a seller will make most of its money and compete for the chance to become the Marketplace Gorilla.

In the Gorilla Game, this is a difficult transition to accomplish. The path from one stage to the next is not a smooth journey. Not every company gets to compete for the grand prize. Instead, only companies that employ a sales approach with a chance of being successful in the mass market will be able to make this crossing. The key to crossing the sea successfully is to select a method of sales that allows the company to (1) sell its product in a profitable manner, (2) ensure that the seller can reach enough prospects to become a viable market leadership candidate, and (3) achieve a sustainable close rate.

Unless the company is a "unicorn" like Slack, which can generate significant revenue without even having a sales force, most other sellers will struggle to cross successfully, due to the standard sales methodologies that exist today. It is next to impossible for a direct seller to sell in a manner that meets the three criteria of Profit, Volume, and Close Rate. Similarly, sellers that try to use third-party distribution arrangements or an inside sales approach will also find it difficult to reach the necessary number of buyers in the mass market to achieve a market leadership position. This means that a majority of technology sellers will eventually fail.

The exceptions to this rule are the enterprises that receive massive amounts of outside financing. Armed with a monetary life preserver, these companies can float to the mainland and happily ignore the realities facing other, less fortunate, sellers. Most will not be in the position to compete for the gorilla spot. At first, life for these companies is not too rough. They simply need to continue to live off the largess of their benefactors. However, for most, the party will not last forever. Once a gorilla is anointed, life will become unpleasant, with falling valuations, unforeseen struggles, and eventual failure.

CrossBorder Solutions, my first start-up software company, ran into this transitional conundrum soon after introducing its software product to the B2B marketplace. The company had developed an offering that was designed for SMEs and could not support an extremely high price. At the same time, the company was using a direct sales force to license its product to prospects. Not only were we losing money on every transaction, we could not work with enough prospects to make significant inroads in the marketplace. We simply did not have the funds necessary to build a large national sales force. This situation left an opening for one of our better-funded competitors to leap ahead of us and begin to obtain real traction in the battle to become the marketplace leader. This was in spite of the fact that we had a first-to-market advantage and our product was more advanced.

Raising venture capital was not possible, unfortunately, and with failure quickly becoming a possibility, CrossBorder Solutions took a sharp left turn and embarked on a radical new path of sales to the business community. As our direct sales force was restricting our profitability and preventing us from making inroads into the mass market, the company instead began relying on web-meeting software as its primary method of dealing with prospects. As the next chapter shows, this technology became the foundation of our new sales approach that allowed the company to transition successfully from the Early Adopters to the mass market, where it had the opportunity to compete for the title of Marketplace Gorilla!

CHAPTER 2

Introduction to a Sales Assembly Line Solution

CREATING A NEW SALES CHANNEL IN THE B2B MARKETPLACE

CrossBorder Solutions was a start-up software company founded in my mother's living room in New York City. It struggled financially after trying to sell a mid-priced product to the SME market using a direct sales force. Moreover, the company was in danger of losing its first go-to-market opportunity to larger, more established competitors. This chapter will describe how developing and implementing a web-meeting sales assembly line allowed a small, undercapitalized company to reach the mass market and obtain a leadership position in an incredibly profitable manner.

CrossBorder Solutions was founded to provide multinational corporations with low-cost software and consulting services that will help companies to determine and document for various regulatory agencies that their goods and services were transferred to related parties at "arm's-length." Prior to this, the only way that companies could prepare the necessary filings was to engage one of the Big Four accounting firms. Due to this lock on the market, these firms were able to charge an exorbitant fee for their services, which left many companies in noncompliance because they could not afford the high fees. CrossBorder Solutions' contention was to automate the solution, giving these smaller enterprises an opportunity to have a viable compliance alternative for a fraction of the traditional cost.

After a three-year development cycle, the company began licensing the software. Following the advice of lawyers, accountants, and other entrepreneurs, the company adopted the standard direct sales force model, as outlined in the book *Crossing the Chasm* by Geoffrey A. Moore. Along with myself, a few salespeople were hired, and with high hopes, we began selling our creation. Initially, this effort was successful. The company was able to work within a tightly defined segment of Early Adopters, and after the first year, the company had landed a couple of dozen clients, established a reasonable pipeline, and started to develop the beginning of a reputation.

While this was initially encouraging, this positive start masked the fact that CrossBorder Solutions was losing money on every transaction due to the outrageously high costs of sale. Moreover, it was clear that using the direct sales methodology ensured that the company would not be able to obtain a market leadership position. This fact was particularly disturbing, as a number of other start-ups and established companies had also just released competitive products. In fact, if we doubled our sales force (and our loss), we still would have only closed a hundred or so clients, which was definitely not the pathway to market domination.

To try and fix this predicament, the company attempted two different approaches. The first was tactical, and consisted of raising the price of the product with the hope this would help the sales operation become profitable. This increase meant the company would now target larger companies that could presumably afford the new price of the offering. While it was cool to be able to say that we had General Electric or American Express as our customers, and their logos certainly looked good on our investor deck, the relief they afforded was relatively short lived.

Selling to these large companies was extremely difficult. It was a challenge to get them to focus on the offer in an expedited manner, which continued to put pressure on the company's financial position. In addition, they were tough negotiators who drove a hard bargain, which negatively impacted the profit margins on each deal. Moreover, once a deal closed, due to the product's high price, each customer was very demanding. The support obligations soon became overwhelming. Finally, the move upstream had another insidious side effect—the competition became aware of the new solution that was being offered to their largest and most important clients. As a result, these large firms suddenly became much more aggressive and even started to develop competing technology solutions. In short order, we abandoned the high-priced, low-volume strategy.

The second approach was to try and forge a selling partnership with an existing seller of related software. Under this scenario, Cross-Border Solutions would not have needed to develop its own sales force and instead would have relied on the third party to distribute the offering. After spending significant time and money on this effort, we still could not reach an acceptable deal. The potential partner was willing to market our software, but it was not willing to provide concrete sales guarantees. This was extremely painful, since during the negotiations there was a lack of focus on building out the sales operation. Consequently, the company found itself in a pretty big hole when the negotiations failed. The takeaway from this terribly upsetting experience was the firm belief that to be successful, it would be necessary to discover a way to sell the product, as there were simply no shortcuts to success.

CrossBorder Solutions needed to find a "new" way to market its products to the Early Majority that would not only be profitable (remember, we did not have VC money behind us, so if we couldn't make money we were out of business) but also allow the company to reach the mass market and achieve a sustainable close rate. It should not be a surprise that the Internet would play a central role in discovering an optimal sales approach. The trick was to find a way to use this technology while selling sophisticated software to the business community.

While selling sophisticated software over the web in a manner similar to selling socks or books was clearly not going to be the company's salvation, we wanted to approximate the two factors that made web selling attractive—it lowered the cost of interacting with prospects and enabled sellers to reach large numbers of prospects rather than focusing on small, defined market segments. However, the approach needed to overcome the fact that business buyers were conditioned to and seemed to be insistent on having some sort of personal interaction with the company's sales representatives. What follows is an overview of our sales approach, as well as a discussion on how it was able to meet the three criteria for a successful sales operation.

1. CAN A SALES ASSEMBLY LINE SELLER ACHIEVE PROFITABILITY?

Desperation pushed us to consider using web-meeting software to conduct our appointments. Using WebEx or other similar products allowed our sales professionals to demonstrate the company's software over the Internet. After many heated discussions with the company's traditionalists who argued that direct sales was the only approach that would work, it was decided that the web-meeting software would be employed as a qualification tool. The thought behind this strategy was if the company could at least weed out the "window shoppers" by using this medium, it could then allocate its scarce direct sales resources to targets that had a higher probability of closing. This approach would presumably lower the costs of sales by eliminating some travel.

This strategy of using web-meeting software to qualify prospects had an immediate positive impact. The company's travel-related expenses fell because fewer overall visits were made, and the close rate associated with on-site visits improved. Quickly, however, another surprising trend became apparent. To the astonishment of almost everyone in the company, a relatively high percentage of prospects, after viewing the presentation and software over the Internet, were willing to purchase the product without any in-person visit at all from the sales professional.

The ability to conduct sales calls using web-meeting software had a radical impact on the underlying costs of distribution, since it dramatically lowered the direct costs of making a sale. It was no longer necessary to spend thousands of dollars traveling to each prospect. Instead, our sales professionals could perform the demo in a specially designed, soundproof demo room, and the only cost of interaction with the prospect was the sales professional's salary for the hour that the appointment took and whatever time was spent on following up with the potential lead. Instead of each appointment costing thousands of dollars, the cost was lowered to a few hundred dollars.

Further improving the profitability of the sales operation was the dramatic increase in appointment production that could occur through the use of web meetings. Since an appointment represented only a one-hour time slot in the day of the individual sales professional, assuming an hour appointment, he or she could theoretically perform eight per day, resulting in forty per week. While this was not an optimal number, as it left too little time for appropriate follow-up, through trial and error it was determined that a sales professional could spend three hours per day performing new appointments. As a web appointment typically took one hour, a sales professional could perform three *new* appointments per day, or sixty per month, and still have enough time to work his or her pipeline appropriately.

This was more than a sixfold increase from what the typical direct sales professional would be able to accomplish.[5]

In the direct sales environment, due to travel and other responsibilities, a sales professional could have never achieved this type of throughput. Similarly, although the inside sales enterprise made strides in the right direction by breaking off the lead-generation function and doubling demo production, these steps were still not enough throughput to transform the company into a profitable venture or one that could conquer the mass market. In both cases, each individual sales professional was not able to spend enough time actually selling. In the web-meeting sales environment, the only way a salesperson could perform so many appointments per day was to flip the sales-to-total-work ratio on its head. Instead of spending four to eight hours per week selling (10 percent to 20 percent), to be able to handle the increase in volume, the web-meeting salesperson needed to spend 85 percent of his or her time on this all-important task.

The key to accomplishing this objective was to employ an advanced level of sales specialization. With this approach, instead of the salesperson performing many functions, if a sales-related task could be accomplished by a less expensive resource, it was removed from the salesperson's purview. For example, similar to an inside sales organization, outbound prospecting was given to a dedicated group of

---

5   The three-appointment rule was not actually the optimal appointment number. In the CrossBorder Solutions environment, each appointment lasted approximately one hour. The sales professional would spend the first fifteen minutes of any demonstration building an initial relationship with the prospect and introducing the company and product by using a PowerPoint presentation. The demonstration was then turned over to the sales engineer, who showed the software and answered any questions that the prospect might have had. During this stage of the demo, the sales professional was largely silent. This changed during the last fifteen minutes of the demonstration, when the sales professional once again became involved and used this time to begin moving the prospect through the initial stages of the sales funnel.

Once this basic cadence was well established, it became clear that having the sales professional sit and do nothing for half the time allocated to the demonstration was extremely inefficient. It should have been possible to have each salesperson perform two demonstrations during each hour demo period. This would have allowed the salesperson to perform *six* demos per day, or 120 per month! Unfortunately, at that time, our internal sales scheduling system could not handle the complexity associated with this approach.

SDRs. Similarly, all customer-related tasks became the responsibility of the separate Customer Success Group. Finally, to minimize the time spent by each sales professional producing correspondence such as proposals and purchase orders, it was much more cost-efficient and effective to hire a group of sales engineers and assistants to undertake this work. The end result of this arrangement was that the salesperson did nothing but sell all day long.

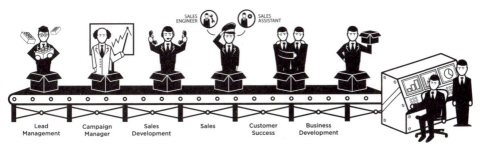

When we adopted this approach, our new sales process began to resemble an assembly line. Once a lead or prospect was identified, it moved through a multistage sales process, which comprised six distinct steps. Each step was staffed by the "right worker"—the individual best suited to perform the activity from an ability *and/or* cost perspective. Sales specialization dramatically increased the throughput or volume of deals each salesperson could work at any given time. In this environment, each salesperson was now able to spend 85 percent of his or her time selling, which equated to thirty-four hours per week, or 1,700 hours per year.

This is an enormous increase when compared to the direct sales and inside sales professional who spent 5/240 and 10/500 hours, respectively.

Moreover, specialization dramatically decreased the costs associated with each transaction. This was because so many of the sales-related tasks were given to a much cheaper resource. There was some concern in the beginning that adding so many professionals to the sales process would lead to a cost-of-sales increase. However, that did not occur, due to the incredible throughput of the individual sales professional. In fact, the cost per closed transaction fell substantially!

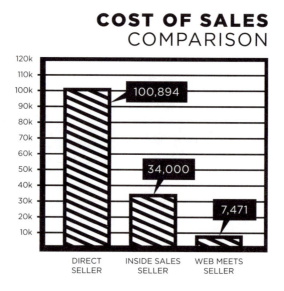

COST OF SALES COMPARISON

The impact was that net revenue grew considerably, and the Cross-Border Solutions financial picture underwent a radical transformation. Instead of the company losing money, each transaction became wildly profitable, to the point that our sales assembly line was throwing off so much cash that the entire company moved into the black. The margins experienced by CrossBorder Solutions were so substantial that the company no longer needed outside funding like most start-ups. Instead, the company funded its internal growth through free cash flow. The end result was that founders and employees were able to hold on to their shares of the company without any dilution and were able to enjoy the proceeds of the sale.

To demonstrate the power of the web-meeting sales assembly line on the profitability of a seller, let's examine the impact this change would have had on SocialFlow. For the purposes of this example, every variable of the model shown on page 33 was held constant with the following exceptions:

1. The direct and indirect travel costs associated with each appointment were completely eliminated.

2. One marketing professional ($45,000 per year), two lead management professionals ($25,000 per year each), four inside sales professionals ($30,000 per year each), two sales assistants ($30,000 per year each), and finally four customer success professionals ($50,000 per year each) were hired, which added approximately $475,000 to the burn of the company.

3. It was assumed that each sales professional could perform up to three new appointments per day.

These changes had a dramatic and startling impact on Social-Flow's financials:

Year 1	Direct Sales	Inside Sales	Sales Assembly Line
Revenue	1,900,000	3,050,000	14,400,000
Cost of Sales	3,882,2000	2,076,000	4,218,000
Net Revenue Sales	(1,982,000)	974,000	10,182,000
Other Costs	12,940,000	6,920,000	14,060,000
Company Net Revenue	(11,280,000)	(3,870,000)	340,000

Year 2	Direct Sales	Inside Sales	Sales Assembly Line
Revenue	3,420,000	5,490,000	25,920,000
Cost of Sales	4,064,400	2,368,800	5,238,000
Net Revenue Sales	(644,400)	3,121,200	20,682,000
Other Costs	13,548,000	7,896,000	17,460,000
Company Net Revenue	(10,128,000)	(2,406,000)	8,460,000

Year 3	Direct Sales	Inside Sales	Sales Assembly Line
Revenue	4,636,000	7,442,000	35,136,000
Cost of Sales	4,210,320	2,603,040	5,238,000
Net Revenue Sales	425,680	4,838,960	29,898,000
Other Costs	14,034,400	8,676,800	17,460,000
Company Net Revenue	(9,398,400)	(1,234,800)	17,676,000

In sum, by dramatically increasing the throughput of each sales professional while reducing the costs of sales, the web-meeting sales assembly line transformed the struggling company into a money-making machine. What is even more important is that SocialFlow was able to accomplish this when selling a mid-priced product rather than an expensive offering. As such, this ability provides B2B technology sellers the chance to select an optimal price point to meet market conditions, rather than simply choosing a high price based on the financial needs of the enterprise.

2. CAN A SALES ASSEMBLY LINE SELLER REACH AND DOMINATE THE MASS MARKET?

Once the profitability question was answered affirmatively, the next question was whether the company could use the sales assembly line to conquer the mass market. Even more important, could CrossBorder Solutions do it quickly enough to vanquish its competitors and become the Marketplace Gorilla?

Conducting appointments and sales specialization over the web allowed the company to increase its appointment production dramatically. However, this improvement would have been for naught if the company could not provide each sales professional with enough leads to keep the sales assembly line working at an optimal level. In a perfect world, it would have been great for CrossBorder Solutions to have been able to generate enough inbound leads to keep the sales professionals fully utilized. Unfortunately, the response rate from various marketing mechanisms we were employing simply could not produce a sufficient number of inbound leads. As a result, the company needed to find a better way to connect potential buyers with the organization.

To resolve this issue, we developed an aggressive outbound call operation made up of junior sales professionals who were cheaper and easier to recruit than the typical account executive. Eventually, we created an entire team of cold-callers. These sales development representatives (SDRs) cold-called prospects all day long and passed "live" leads, called opportunities, on to the sales professionals, who then demonstrated the product to the prospects over the web and tried to close them. Leads that did not close in a reasonable amount of time were removed from the sales professional's "queue" and were put back into the prospect-lead database where they would be cold-called again and again until they decided to reschedule an appointment and start the process all over again. It was a constant running joke that clients licensed our software just to stop the SDRs from calling them!

Originally, the sales development group was part of the sales team.

However, when it became apparent that the individual sales professionals were overly influencing the callers' behavior, this group was pulled out and became part of the marketing group. In a similar vein, at first, each sales development professional was teamed up with a salesperson, as we thought this would be a great way to onboard and train the junior professional. But it became apparent that this structure was fundamentally unfair to the sales professional. For example, if the sales development professional was underperforming, the salesperson would not have a sufficient number of opportunities to work. Evaluating each salesperson objectively also became difficult. Therefore, this structure was eliminated, and leads developed by the sales development professional were distributed to the sales team, using a formula that ensured statistical and numerical equality.

When the sales development team was first formed, each member of the team was expected to make approximately forty phone calls and schedule one appointment every other day. This output was clearly not enough to keep our hungry sales team busy. It was necessary to find a way to improve the group's production substantially. After carefully examining their daily tasks, it seemed that the callers spent an inordinate amount of time "picking and pecking" through their pipeline to find the "right" name to call. To alleviate this systemic bottleneck, a feature was added to the internal sales system that intelligently provided each professional with the proper name to call. To increase efficiency, the system did not randomly select this name but instead used a sophisticated algorithm to figure out which name in the pipeline was the optimal prospect to call at that given moment. A wide variety of factors were considered, including time of day and the importance of the call. Including this feature resulted in a dramatic increase in the number of dials each sales development representative made each day. While increasing the number of dials to over one hundred helped, it was still not enough to generate the appointments necessary to keep the sales professionals fully utilized.

We initially considered using an automatic dialer, in an attempt to raise the volume of calls even higher. However, prospects noticed the delay in picking up the phone, so a substantial number of potential customers ended the call before our sales representative could get a chance to pitch. As it was getting difficult to increase the number of dials, we needed to examine and implement methods to improve the close rate of the sales development professionals. For example, direct marketing efforts were tightly integrated with the team's cold-calling activities. Traditionally, direct marketing is undertaken to brand a product or company and to generate inbound leads. At first, these mass-market efforts were quite successful. Thousands of emails or direct mail pieces would be sent out to prospects, which would typically generate a 2 percent response rate—the industry standard for a moderately successful outbound campaign. Moreover, since the prospects self-selected, this was a highly efficient and effective way to identify prospects.

Unfortunately, while this effort was initially successful, each subsequent marketing campaign got a lower and less enthusiastic response. However, when a prospect who received an email or direct mail was called and *reached* by a sales development professional within a day of receiving the communication, the close rate for that prospect rose by over 50 percent. Based on this observation, instead of continuing to undertake mass marketing campaigns, which were extremely expensive and ultimately wasteful, the company only sent out what could be called by the sales development team within one day of receipt. To effectuate this approach, the intelligent calling feature of our sales automation system ensured that the right names were presented to our callers at the right time and at the optimal frequency. This technique helped increase the close rate of the sales development team in a dramatic manner without any related increase in costs.

While tightly tying outbound calling and outbound marketing together was certainly helpful, A/B testing was a true game changer.

Under this approach, the company tested two different versions of an outbound calling process. Half of the prospects being called were presented with one option (known as the control) and the other half of the prospects were presented with another version (the variation). The version that led to a higher conversion or close rate would be rolled out to the entire sales development team to be used with a wider pool of prospects. Over time, many of the aspects of the sales development process were evaluated and tested. Examples of A/B testing included:

- **Script Analysis.** Before releasing a call script to the sales development professionals, it was carefully tested against our standard message, which allowed management to determine scientifically which calling approach worked best for different types of buyers. For example, through testing, we discovered that a pitch that stressed our support services worked better or had a higher close rate when it was used in conjunction with potential female buyers. Similarly, a script stressing cost reduction rather than time savings worked better with CFOs.

- **Offer Analysis.** Early on, testing revealed that including a "special" offer in the standard pitch dramatically improved the close rate. Using offers became an even more powerful incentive to schedule a demonstration after the testing showed that different offers worked better with certain buyers.

- **Marketing Collateral Analysis.** A wide range of direct marketing approaches were constantly tested. For example, before sending and engaging in a mass mail or email campaign, a small run would be conducted with half the recipients receiving a market communication with message A. The other half would receive one with message B. The message with a higher close rate would be employed on a wider basis. Not only was the message tested, but the type of piece and the look and feel of the marketing collateral were analyzed as well.

- **Processes Analysis.** A wide range of processes were tested to determine their impact on the sales development close rate. For example, having the sales development representative remind the prospect of an upcoming demonstration dramatically improved the performance rate. Similarly, asking for permission to call the prospect back rather than just saying "thanks for your time" at the end of a successful call improved the chances of eventually scheduling a demonstration.

This type of testing took the guesswork out of the sales development process and enabled data-informed decisions that shifted the conversations from "we think" to "we know." It allowed management to customize and optimize the experience with the prospect in order to gain a desired outcome. This approach made the cold-calling process much more effective and led to a dramatic improvement in the close rates. Finally, with this method and others, the inside sales team was able to schedule an appropriate number of appointments to ensure the sales team was fully utilized.

In sum, cold-calling by a separate and distinct team turned out to be an amazing "connector" that allowed the company to have personalized and optimized one-on-one conversations with an incredibly large number of prospects in the mass market. The bottom-line impact of this approach was that the number of appointments dramatically increased. In a matter of months, CrossBorder Solutions went from performing twenty demonstrations per month to performing hundreds. Moreover, while the number of overall appointments was higher, the quality of these appointments did not decrease. This is directly attributable to the fact that the company was now in the position to reach and interact with the "right" type of targets contained in the mass market. With these numbers, the company was not only in the position to play but to win the Gorilla Game.

Let's return to the SocialFlow example to demonstrate the impact

ALWAYS BE TESTING!

Using A/B Testing to Take the Guesswork out of
Sales Optimization

A/B testing allows seller to scientifically test two different versions of a sales
process simultaneously to determine which will lead to a higher close rate.

THE SECRET SAUCE OF B2B SALES

Figuring out what makes a prospect license your solution is the
holy grail of B2B sales. Using artificial intelligence to discern what
factors influence buying decisions will dramatically improve a
seller's close rate which will lead to higher, more profitable
revenue.

WHAT CAN YOU TEST?

 OFFERS
Discover which deal
terms drive sales

 PRICE
Find out the impact
of raising price

 SCRIPTS
Uncover which
message works best

 **MARKETING
COLLATERAL**
Discover which approach
generates more leads

 PROCESSES
Ascertain which
actions drive results

 DEMOS
Learn which style is
more convincing

62%

38%

HOW TO KNOW, NOT GUESS

 Pick Variable
to Test

 Determine Lead
Source & Quantity

 Evaluate
Close Rate

the web-meeting sales assembly line had in reaching the mass market. Using a direct sales force of four professionals who scheduled their own appointments, SocialFlow was able to perform thirty-two new appointments per month, or 384 annually. If the company achieved a close rate of 10 percent, this would mean that the company would have closed approximately thirty-eight deals. Similarly, using the inside sales approach, the company was only able to generate sixty-one deals. With these relatively low numbers, it is doubtful the company could obtain a market leadership position.

OF 1ST APPOINTMENTS
PER WEEK

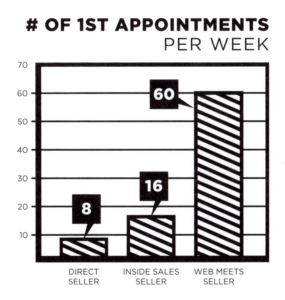

However, if the sales assembly line methodology was employed, the sales force of four sales professionals would have performed 240 per month, or 2,880 yearly demonstrations. Assuming that the same close rate was achieved, the company would close 288 deals. If the company hired twenty professionals, the company would have performed 1,600 demonstrations per month, or 19,200 appointments per year, and closed approximately 1,920 deals. Moreover, SocialFlow would have been able to do this without raising the additional funds necessary to build a mega sales force. Now, for the first time, our fictional company was able to reach its client acquisition goals and dominate the mass market!

3. CAN THE WEB-MEETING SELLER ACHIEVE A SUSTAINABLE CLOSE RATE?

Up to this point, the sales assembly line has dramatically bested either the direct or inside sales approach in terms of profitability and the ability to reach the mass market. These two factors would mean absolutely nothing if the prospects were not inclined to purchase the software using this unique sales methodology. When CrossBorder Solutions first began using the approach, there was a fair amount of consternation and belief that we would not be able to achieve the close rate associated with the direct sales method. Happily, various strategies were developed that made web-meeting sales better approximate an in-person appointment, and with this shift, any initial degradation in close rate *completely* disappeared. In fact, over time, by introducing the improvements listed below, the company was able to achieve the same close rate typically enjoyed by a direct sales force, long believed to be the gold standard.

Benefit One: Multiple Appointments

In a traditional sales environment, to control the direct and indirect costs of sale, sellers normally tightly control the number and location of salesperson visits to any given prospect. This limitation can have a negative impact on the close rate, because the buyer might not be able to build the necessary confidence in the offering.

In the web-meeting sales assembly line environment, as travel was eliminated, it was economically feasible to conduct as many appointments as the prospect desired without having a negative impact on the bottom line. In fact, at CrossBorder Solutions, it was standard operating procedure to conduct an initial demonstration of the solution and then to schedule at least one follow-up demonstration immediately, to explore any issues raised during the first meeting.

Benefit Two: Multiple Decision Makers in Multiple Locations

In the modern business environment, when trying to make a sale, it is not unusual for decision influencers and makers to be located in multiple locations. In a direct sales environment, it is often necessary to travel to meet these disparately located professionals. This process can dramatically add to the number of visits and therefore the expense (in time and dollars) of the sales effort. Often, sellers restrict their sales professionals from this type of location hopping. In this case, the prospect is responsible for getting all the right people in a room, or more likely, some people are left out and not able to meet face-to-face with the salesperson. This lack of inclusiveness can reduce the seller's effectiveness and the associated close rate.

In a web-meeting sales environment, location becomes a nonissue. When conducting a web meeting, multiple participants from different locations can join a scheduled meeting at the same time. While a single meeting was the most efficient method, it was fairly painless to conduct multiple individual web meetings. The ability to be inclusive helped to dramatically improve the close rate when selling to corporations where decision makers were spread all over a large geographic territory.

Benefit Three: Shortened Sales Cycle

A sales truism is that the longer the sales cycle, the greater the chance the deal will fall apart. This is because any lapse in time provides the opportunity for unexpected issues, both related and unrelated to the sale, to develop. In a traditional sales situation, one thing that commonly lengthens the cycle is the time it takes to identify and schedule an in-person meeting time convenient both for the sales professional and the prospect. The difficulty surrounding this effort is magnified when multiple parties need to be included in the evaluation and decision-making process. When these parties are located in different jurisdictions, the sales process can almost grind to a halt, dramatically lowering the close rate.

Web-meeting sales almost completely remove this roadblock. From the sales professional's perspective, since there were approximately forty "appointment" slots to work with per week, it was relatively easy to find a time convenient for the prospect. From the prospect's perspective, since the sales call was being conducted over the Internet, it became much easier to schedule appointments with multiple parties, as they simply had to log in to a website rather than travel to the central location. All of the above factors meant that the sales cycle could be shortened dramatically, which also had a positive impact on the overall close rate.

Benefit Four: Use of Sales Engineers

Depending on the complexity of the solution being sold, it is often preferable to have sales engineers—individuals who are industry or product experts—assist the salespeople in demoing the product and explaining its benefits. Since these individuals are often relatively expensive professionals who are a scarce resource in the traditional sales environment, it is normally impossible to send them on the road to every prospect. As a result, their time is strictly rationed, and they are used only with the "best" leads or largest sales opportunities. This constraint certainly has a negative impact on the traditional seller's close rate.

The single most powerful benefit of employing a web-meeting sales platform was that it became possible to have a sales engineer on *every* single sales call. In fact, at CrossBorder Solutions, once the sales professional set the stage at the start of the web meeting, the sales engineer conducted most of the product demonstration. This approach transformed a sales call into a detailed conversation between industry experts, which helped the company build an enormous amount of credibility when conducting a web meeting. In addition, the fact that the sales engineer was able to answer questions and respond to concerns in real time helped keep the sales process moving along nicely. The extensive use of sales engineers had a dramatic impact on CrossBorder Solutions' close rate and was in fact one of the keys to the success of the sales assembly line operation.

Benefit Five: Analysis of Sales Data

Due to the limited number of appointments a traveling sales force can conduct and the fact that each salesperson likely performs many roles in this environment, it is difficult, if not impossible, to analyze a direct sales operation mathematically. These impediments are not present in the web-meeting sales assembly line environment, which gives the seller the ability to analyze the company's sales performance statistically by combing data that was a by-product of the internal sales management system.

The CrossBorder Solutions system captured a wide range of data that was carefully mined to gain greater insight on a wide variety of topics. This mathematical information allowed the company to evaluate the sales professionals and the sales process itself, and even to predict certain sales results. By tweaking the sales process based on these results, it was possible to eliminate inefficiencies and fine-tune the sales approach, which directly led to an increase in the close rate as well.

BUILDING A STABLE BRIDGE

THE CONTESTANT

Seller Employing Web-Meeting Sales Assembly Line

| Lead Management | Campaign Manager | Sales Development | Sales | Customer Success | Business Development |

With a web-meeting seller, every step in the sales process will be handled by the "best" resources from either a cost or ability standpoint. As such, multiple professionals will play a role in the sales process.

85% TIME SPENT SELLING

SALES APPROACH DETAILS

Multiple Meetings · Shortened Sales Cycle

The Use of Sales Engineers · Analysis of Sales Data

PROFITABLITY

A web-meeting seller will only use web-meeting software to interact with the prospect.

SALES VOLUME

By using web-meeting software and by employing labor specialization, sales professionals can dramatically increase throughput.

CLOSE RATE

By using the features that are unique to web-meeting sales, at a basic level, a web-meeting seller can meet or even exceed close rates achieved by a Direct Seller.

THE RESULT: Will the Bridge Stand?	Formula for Sales Success		
	PROFITABILITY	VOLUME	CLOSE RATE
	✔	✔	✔

4. CONCLUSION

By adopting the sales assembly line approach, CrossBorder Solutions met the three criteria of a successful sales operation: the ability to sell a mid-priced product in a profitable manner, reach a large percentage of the potential market, and achieve a reasonable close rate. The sales approach enabled the company to cross from the Early Adopter segment into the mass market and begin marketing to the Early Majority. Relatively quickly, the company was able to land a few hundred clients. Even more important, a number of competitors dropped out of the competition, as they could not navigate the crossing in a successful manner.

Surviving and successfully making the transition to the mainland was certainly a positive development. The company was finally in the position to compete for the market leadership position. However, everyone understood that the third stage of the Gorilla Game was going to be even more difficult. Unfortunately, the company was not the only seller to make the crossing successfully. Two other enterprises also garnered a degree of initial market acceptance and were making a run to be the market leader. The fight to become the Marketplace Gorilla was not going to be an easy one. Our most feared competitor was Corptax, which was the second-largest tax software company in the United States, with thousands of clients and over $300 million in revenue. The second competitor, KPMG, was one of the largest accounting firms in the world, with sales over $2 billion. If a bookie was going to give odds on the upcoming "battle royal," clearly CrossBorder Solutions would have been the underdog by a wide margin! This was especially the case considering that the company was still an unfunded, struggling start-up with less than $10 million in revenue.

However, CrossBorder Solutions had a secret weapon. Due to the large number of demos that could be performed by a relatively small number of sales professionals, our sales assembly line was able to create and project a footprint many times larger than what could be accomplished by our competitors, who were still primarily relying on a direct sales force. This type of enhanced force projection served as a multiplier that evened the scales and at least gave the company a fighting chance to win the title of Marketplace Gorilla.

CHAPTER 3

Supercharging the Performance of a Sales Assembly Line

HOW THE PLATFORM DRAMATICALLY IMPROVED THE CLOSE RATE OF THE ENTERPRISE

It would be a mistake to assume that one day CrossBorder Solutions discovered this new way to sell, and suddenly, the company was one of those über-successful, high-flying start-ups profiled in *Fast Company*. The company was still an undercapitalized concern dealing daily with all the problems and issues that typically plague a start-up concern. Moreover, while it made the successful crossing into the Early Majority, the company still had two formidable competitors that seemed to be in the fight for the long haul and were willing to do almost anything to ensure that our insurgency would not survive. These competitors had great reputations, huge existing client bases, and, compared to us, unlimited amounts of money to spend on this effort. While we were elated that we had survived the "initial" test, there was the real fear that after all this hard work and effort, Cross-Border Solutions would be relegated to being a monkey at best, or at worst, another B2B failure statistic.

The sales assembly line platform was clearly going to be our salvation. It had allowed us to stem the financial bleed. Moreover, the free cash flow it generated provided the company with the resources to begin to scale its sales and support organization without raising outside capital. Surprisingly, the platform did much more. What was originally conceived simply as a sales strategy unexpectedly morphed into a catalyst that changed the underlying business structure of our young enterprise and helped dictate the direction the company would take as it matured. Specifically, the platform made it possible (1) to successfully sell to the entire mass market rather than employ the standard segmentation strategy and (2) to gain tight control over the sales process. Taken together, the company's sales assembly line was able to avoid many of the pitfalls that typically trip up an emerging enterprise. More important, these factors helped it achieve a close rate that has rarely been experienced before in B2B technology sales. With this, CrossBorder Solutions was in the game and ready to compete to become the Marketplace Gorilla.

1. BENEFITS OF SELLING TO THE ENTIRE MARKET

Traditionally, B2B sellers have been taught to enter the mass market using a segmentation strategy. First, the seller would work within a small segment, and once dominance was achieved, the company would move on to a related segment. This pathway was known as puddle jumping, and eventually, when this was done enough times, the puddles would merge together and the seller would find itself to be the market leader. This tried-and-true strategy made sense when using a direct sales force. Due to throughput limitations of the sales professional, a small segment with a limited number of targets is all that a direct seller could handle. This artificial constraint was removed when the sales assembly line was employed. With the assembly line method, the company was not forced to work within small, defined segments. Instead, it is able to think of the market as a single unit, which provides a number of benefits.

Benefit One: Identifying Early Adopters

Conventional wisdom holds that 10 percent of a typical business marketplace is made up of buyers who can be classified as Early Adopters. These buyers purchase new products in spite of the flaws inherent in a new offering. A critical aspect of a new product launch is to identify and close these companies, because they provide the foundation for future growth. Unfortunately, employing the traditional sales segmentation strategy makes it hard to identify and sell to a large portion of these buyers. For example, if a selected segment comprises only one hundred companies, then there would be only ten companies that would fall into this classification. Even if the company achieved an unrealistic 20 percent close rate, the seller would likely be able to close only two of these companies.

When segments were ignored, the problem of identifying and closing Early Adopters was minimized. Since the sales assembly line approach was such a high-volume sales operation, this allowed us to reach these golden nuggets in short order. In fact, our relatively small sales development operation was able to reach and identify the companies willing to consider an immature product from an unestablished vendor. The ability to work with Early Adopters dramatically improved our close rate, especially in the early days of the enterprise.

Benefit Two: Market Feedback

When employing a tight segmentation strategy, it is possible that the seller will become overly dependent on the opinions of the prospects located in the first few segments. As a practical matter, in many cases, this initial feedback will determine the direction the new offering will take. However, there is an overwhelming possibility that the guide-posts established by this small sample of data points are not going to be indicative of what the whole rest of the mass market wants or needs. Often, the end result of feedback from only a small sample is that the traditional seller will suddenly find that it developed a solution not acceptable to a majority of the companies in the mass market. If the solution is unacceptable to the majority, the forward momentum of the seller operating in the Early Majority segment can stall, and other companies with a more suitable product offering can leap ahead in the race for market dominance.

For our company, selling to the entire market almost completely eliminated this market dislocation issue. Due to the volume of appointments and therefore the sheer number of one-to-one cus-tomer touches the sales assembly line platform generated, the company obtained a tremendous amount of market feedback in a relatively short amount of time. In this way, the sales platform served as a giant market research mechanism that helped our development operation fine-tune its offerings (e.g., features and marketing mes-sages) so they closely matched what the overall market was looking for in a solution. This ability to quickly determine product/market fit improved our overall close rate.

Benefit Three: Opaqueness

By definition, a segment is a small group of companies that can com-municate with one another. As such, when working within a tightly defined segment, everything the seller does is exposed to a great deal of scrutiny from the rest of the segment participants. It is extremely hard, if not impossible, to hide anything from these interested observ-ers who are waiting to see the results of the "trial" before making their own decision on how to proceed with the new product or service.

By focusing on the entire market rather than a single segment, the sales assembly line methodology helps wrap the seller in an invisibility cloak that reduces the transparency of its operations to the marketplace as a whole. This ability to "hide" is helpful in a number of ways.

- It is inevitable that when trying to conquer a new market with a new product, mistakes—some serious—are going to be made. In a traditional environment, these "issues" would become known to the other segment participants, and depending on the seriousness of the problems, a typical company could find itself irreparably harmed within the segment. In the CrossBorder Solutions' sales assembly line environment, since it was unlikely that most of the companies contained in the mass market knew one another, adherence to the methodology made it less likely that any initial problems would become widely known.

- When visiting clients face-to-face, it is extremely difficult to hide the fact that the seller is an immature concern, which lowers the buyer's confidence in the solution. Selling via the web-meeting sales platform helps hide this fact, since the buyer never meets the salesperson in person. In our case, the only window into the company was the public face presented via the marketing communications and online appointments. We were able to manipulate our image easily to make the prospect believe it was dealing with a much larger, more established organization.

- When selling to a small, tightly defined segment, likely everyone in the segment knows exactly the price paid as well as the exact terms surrounding the deal. This situation means that a traditional selling company needs to be fairly consistent in its pricing strategy, even though the result will be lost deals or money left on the table. However, when using the sales assembly line, given the fact that our prospects in the mass market likely did not know one another, it was possible to forgo a strict pricing plan and instead price on a customer-by-customer basis. This flexibility led to a significantly higher customer acquisition rate and the ability to grab more revenue overall.

- References are the lifeblood of any young concern. When working within a tightly defined segment, companies serving as references are generally reluctant to say anything to other segment participants other than the complete and unvarnished truth. This is often because they are uncomfortable lying to peers they interact with regularly. However, this compunction to be brutally honest does not exist when references are speaking with people they don't know and will not likely speak with again. As such, in the sales assembly line environment, references who were our strong supporters seemed more apt to gloss over problems and issues with people they didn't know well, which led to a higher close rate.

Benefit Four: Competitive Response

Just as all the prospects contained in a tightly defined segment know exactly what is happening (the good, the bad, and the ugly) with a new product or service, existing vendors in the segment know everything as well. In fact, working in this type of small-ball environment is akin to providing the seller's game plan to its competitors complete with a nice bow tied around it and an easy-to-read instruction manual. This provides competitors with an enormous opportunity to disrupt the adoption of the new offering by the segment participants. Specifically, with this information, competitors are in a better position to craft more advantageous deals, strategically pick apart the new offering, and highlight potential issues to prospects. In addition, and perhaps most important, they are able to marshal their resources more efficiently, thereby helping them to provide a more effective, coordinated response to the new market interloper.

This competitive advantage was muted if not entirely eliminated when we pursued a mass market strategy. Since the market we were attacking was so large and diverse, it was extremely difficult for our competitors to gain an understanding of what was actually happening in the field. Without this firsthand knowledge, the overall competitive response was haphazard, inefficient, and ineffective. In many ways, our sales assembly line operation was akin to a small guerilla force or insurgency able to make successful surgical strikes against a larger, more established adversary and leave the competitor flat-footed.

2. BENEFITS OF GREATER COMMAND AND CONTROL

The previous section demonstrated how selling to the entire market can help the sales assembly line seller improve its close rate. Playing an equally important role in raising the close rate is how the platform helps management tightly control its operations so they function optimally.

Benefit Five: Discovering and Implementing Best Practices

One of the by-products of a sales assembly line is that an enormous amount of data will be collected on every aspect of the sales process. Using various methods of statistical analyses, such as A/B testing, the seller can determine what factors positively influence a sale. With this knowledge, it should be possible for the company to develop a series of best practices that, if implemented, will improve the team's close rate. Unfortunately, that is often a big "if" in the traditional sales environment, as good salespeople are notoriously independent. One way we ensured that best practices were followed was to put into place defined sales "plays," which were a series of defined sales tasks and steps that should be followed based on the prospect or on an opportunity's unique circumstances. Gently pushing CrossBorder Solutions' sales professionals in the right direction helped ensure that best practices were followed and led to a higher close rate.

Benefit Six: Better Evaluation of Sales Talent

In a traditional sales situation, it normally takes a few quarters to determine whether a sales professional is going to work out. In cases where the professional is proven to be ineffective, this delay can be expensive from two perspectives. One, valuable leads are being burned during this time, and two, a new replacement is not being hired, which only elongates the pain of failure. This is not the case in a sales assembly line environment.

Because our company randomly distributed leads and opportunities to the sales team, we were able to statistically analyze the sales data to objectively evaluate each team member's performance. This allowed management to quickly determine whether a salesperson was going to be successful in the sales environment. For example, if a salesperson had a close rate after the first quarter of 5 percent and the historical data showed that new sales professionals on average enjoy a 12 percent initial close rate, this indicated that the new salesperson was probably not going to make it and should be immediately replaced. Lessening the number of wasted leads and replacing the failing professional quickly resulted in an overall higher close rate.

Benefit Seven: Early Issue Identification

One of the most challenging aspects of properly supervising a fast-growing staff of sales professionals is that unexpected problems seem to crop up at the most inopportune time and place. If it were possible to anticipate or at least catch these flare-ups early in their development, the transition into the mass market would undoubtedly be smoother. However, based on the distributed nature of a direct sales force, management traditionally has had trouble staying in front of potential issues and more often than not tends to deal with them after they become crises. Of course, dealing with issues after they become serious problems lowers the close rate of the sales organization.

While the web-meeting sales assembly line cannot eliminate all the "gotchas," by regularly poring over the wide range of data generated from the platform on a daily, monthly, and yearly basis, it was possible to look for blips and variances that might have signaled a potential problem in the making. In this manner, the sales assembly line functioned as an early warning system that allowed management to anticipate and deal with potential issues before they turned into true problems. Minimizing or even completely eliminating the issues that would normally have an impact on the performance of the sales team was a powerful way to raise the close rate of the organization. The following example from CrossBorder Solutions illustrates how powerful it was to gain this type of insight.

> The company had just come off a great year. December sales were unusually strong, and more important, the pipeline remained fertile and management felt comfortable that we would be able to extend and build on our winning streak into the following year. However, when we looked at the data generated by the sales platform at the end of January, we noticed that a few important key performance indicators (e.g., proposal rates and closing call rates) were starting to slip slightly when compared against historical data. While the numbers were nothing major at this point, they did attract the attention of the management team, and we decided to watch carefully to see if a trend was developing. Surprisingly, in February, the numbers declined even more. It is important to

note that at this point, our forecasts were still accurate and sales remained strong. However, the numbers told management that a negative trend was quickly developing, and our automatic internal forecasts began to adjust downward to take into account the changing situation.

Following this development, the management team went into overdrive to try and pin down what in the sales process had changed to account for the downward trend. Examining the data generated from the system with a fine-tooth comb, we concluded that something new was happening at the demonstration stage of the sales process. With this information, we knew where to look and started to listen to tapes of every demo conducted over the past month and compare them to recordings made in the previous quarter, when the close rates were higher. After listening to approximately fifty sales calls, it became clear that the sales pitch had changed ever so slightly. In fact, the leadership of the sales team did not even realize the change had occurred. Of course, the sales team was instructed to return to their "old ways," and once they did, the various indicators went right back up as expected.

Without the ability to collect, disseminate, and analyze this data, there is a high likelihood the company would not have realized anything was wrong until it missed sales targets at the end of the first quarter and then again in the second quarter (the shortfall in the first quarter would have been written off as a letdown from the strong fourth). However, the system permitted the company, in real time, to identify a small but serious issue before it had any meaningful impact on its revenue stream.

This type of situation replayed itself over and over again in a wide variety of areas. Being able to identify and rectify issues up front made an enormous difference as the company competed to become the Marketplace Gorilla.

Benefit Eight: Quicker Reaction Time

The path to market domination is fraught with danger. These threats are often amplified by a traditional sales force, since its distributed nature makes it hard to react quickly to developing situations. Nothing slows down reaction times more than differing travel schedules, which make it extremely difficult, if not impossible, to pull the sales team together in one place on a regular basis to provide them with instructions on how to deal with evolving situations. Further aggravating this state of affairs is the fact that once changes are rolled out, it is hard to ensure that the sales team is adopting the "new" strategies.

A key component of a well-functioning sales system is the ability to act with a sense of urgency in a coordinated, controlled manner. Selling via the sales assembly line approach helped us in this regard because the lack of travel meant our sales professionals were able to meet and discuss intelligence gathered from prospect interactions in real time. Based on these meetings, changes were proposed, and if A/B testing bore out the predicted outcome, modifications to the sales process were quickly implemented on a team-wide basis. Furthermore, once changes were enacted, it was possible to (1) ensure they were being applied consistently by the individual sales professionals and (2) continually monitor the impact of the change on the sales process, using the data analysis techniques previously discussed. This ability to turn on a dime and react with lightning speed was a powerful competitive advantage that helped raise the close rate.

Benefit Nine: Improved Onboarding

When selling a new product or service, practice makes perfect. Even the most experienced sales professional needs a fair amount of time to ramp up in a new sales environment. Until this learning curve is scaled, the professional will have a lower close rate. As any delay can quickly become a potent enemy, it is critical for management to accelerate this learning process. However, this is difficult to do in the traditional sales environment. Typically, after some initial training, the sales professional is expected to work independently and, to a large degree, figure out what works and what does not work. This trial-and-error learning process is ineffective and expensive and lowers the overall close rate.

In our sales assembly line environment, the onboarding process was much more efficient. First, since each line worker was only doing one specific task, it was much easier to train and have them become quickly proficient. Second, due to the high volume of leads coursing through the system, each sales professional was in the position to gain a lot of practice in a short amount of time. In addition, as travel was eliminated, a manager, or even a senior sales professional, was included on every initial appointment and was able to work with the new sales professional to train and evaluate his or her demo and closing skills. Similarly, since a sales engineer—a professional who knew the product and the industry—also participated in each demonstration, the new salesperson was able concentrate his or her efforts on improving selling skills, rather than learning the product. Finally, because the process was so tightly scripted and controlled, it was much easier to teach a new professional what worked and what did not. All of the above factors helped the seller to scale in a more efficient manner and maintain its close rate even when new staff joined the team.

Benefit Ten: Improved Training

In the traditional sales environment, it is incredibly expensive to provide sales training because it is necessary to pull the sales professionals in from the road and to halt selling for a time. Often, sellers are reluctant to do so, and over time, this lack of extensive training will negatively impact the close rate of the seller. It also makes it harder for a sales organization to retain salespeople, as ongoing professional development is certainly a component of job satisfaction.

Due to its underlying structure, the sales assembly line at Cross-Border Solutions was a constant learning environment. As every interaction with a prospect occurred online, it was possible for management to spend significant time with each sales resource to improve their performance. Moreover, the online nature of the platform meant that every interaction with a prospect, opportunity, or client was electronically recorded, and the recordings were organized into libraries of good and bad cold calls, good and bad demonstrations, and closing calls. This enabled the sales team to hear for themselves what worked and gave them something to emulate. This had a positive impact on the organization's close rate.

Benefit Eleven: Minimizing the Impact of Professional Turnover

Turnover in any sales organization is a fact of life. The Bridge Group has estimated that the average turnover rate in the software industry approaches 35 percent per year! It stands to reason that this number will be significantly higher in enterprises selling a new product. Turnover is always an extremely painful event that has a negative impact on the overall close rate of the seller because the deals the departing professional was working on are often lost when the person leaves the company.

In a traditional setting, a sales professional who leaves typically sets off a domino effect. First, there is an immediate attempt to pore over the pipeline of the professional who is leaving in an attempt to "save" the prospects that had the greatest chance of closing. Often, it is not an easy task to make this determination with any degree of accuracy, as the data is often suspect. Typically, management would give these prospects to other sales professionals in the organization.

However, since it is likely that these professionals are already working on their own deals, these pickups often get short shrift.

Second, there is the longer-term issue of how to deal with the territory that belonged to the recently departed professional. One option, if logistically possible, would be to have other sales professionals cover the territory until someone new is found. This is not ideal, though, because salespeople will often not properly work on something they know will soon be taken away. Another option, often considered when the territory is not especially fertile, is to let it lie fallow until a new resource can be hired and trained. The obvious impact of this is that sales revenue will fall by the amount that was expected to be generated from this section of the marketplace. If the territory cannot be ignored, another option is to move another professional into the space permanently. This of course leaves a hole someplace else and magnifies the negative revenue repercussions. Suffice it to say that none of these options are particularly attractive, which is why turnover is so incredibly damaging to the close rate and revenue goals of the company.

While turnover in a web-meeting sales assembly line environment is never a pleasant experience, the platform mitigates the impact of the loss in a number of ways. First, due to the data being collected on each prospect, the process of identifying the prospects that are "live" is more efficient and accurate. Second, using our company as an example, the lack of territories meant that any existing and new leads/ opportunities were permanently distributed to the existing sales force. Finally, and perhaps most important, any of our new leads/ opportunities were simply reallocated among the remaining sales professionals on the line without any impact on the organization. As such, eliminating these turnover pain points had a dramatic increase in the overall close rate.

WINNING THE BATTLE FOR THE
MASS MARKET

SUPERCHARGING THE CLOSE RATE

Shortened
Sales Cycle

Better Market
Feedback

Less Dependence
on a Few Clients

Opaqueness or the
Ability to Hide
Problems from
Companies

Quicker Competitive
Response

A/B Testing of
Sales Processes

Better Supervision of
the Sales Staff

More Accurate Sales
Forecasting

Early Issue
Identification

Quicker Reaction
Time

Improved Onboarding

Improved Training

Minimizing Impact
of Professional
Turnover

$$= \text{CLOSE RATE } 18\%$$

By using a variety of features that are unique to the web-meeting sales assembly line, a sales assembly line seller is able to significantly increase its close rate. When combined with the dramatically higher sales throughput, this allows a web-meeting seller to reach and close more than 10X the number of clients. This type of force multiplier will help the web-meeting to dominate and conquer the chosen technology markets and become the undisputed Marketplace Gorilla.

3. CONCLUSION

At the beginning of the book we outlined three criteria that are the hallmarks of a successful sales operation. The web-meeting sales assembly line approach, employed by CrossBorder Solutions, met these principles and resulted in the company successfully transitioning from the Early Adopters to the Early Majority market. While crossing the bridge to the mainland was certainly cause for celebration, the fact that the company was pitted against two formidable competitors made the ensuing battle for the hearts and minds of the mass market a challenge.

It was initially satisfying to see the company was able to achieve a close rate that approximated the figure that would have been attained if a direct sales approach had been employed. Surprisingly, the platform became even more powerful as time passed. Its ability to deal with the entire market at once and to improve the underlying daily operations of the sales force helped the close rate to keep ticking upward. Within two years, the close rate for the company's first product rose to 18 percent, which is much higher than the average B2B seller experiences in the normal course of business.

When this achievement was combined with the continued improvement of the throughput of the sales team, the company went on a growth tear, closing hundreds of deals per year profitably. The fact that our competitors had better software, better support services, and were certainly better funded made absolutely no difference. They could not keep up with our sales progress, and within two years, both of the company's main competitors became marginal players who simply serviced their legacy clients. The web-meeting sales assembly line platform propelled the company to become the undisputed Marketplace Gorilla. With this designation, CrossBorder Solutions was able to raise its product price to $75,000 per year, grew at a 50 percent year-over-year rate, and experienced 50 percent operating margins until it was sold to Thomson Reuters for $80 million.

CHAPTER 4

The Financial Impact of a Sales Assembly Line

THE PRECEDING SECTIONS OF THIS book demonstrated how a sales assembly line seller can not only compete for the title of Marketplace Gorilla but also hands-down win the competition. When our fictional company SocialFlow returned to shore and replaced its direct sales force with a high-velocity, web-meeting sales assembly line, the company was able to hyperscale and change its fortunes. Below is a final scorecard of the results.

This summary makes it abundantly clear that employing the web-meeting sales assembly line approach is a magical, transformative solution. It has the power to take a technology company struggling to survive and turn it into a high-growth, profit-making sales engine. Specifically, by lowering the costs of distribution, increasing its throughput, and improving the close rate, this methodology can help a seller to not only survive but thrive. Armed with this understanding, we can turn to the next section of the book, which illuminates the inner workings of the sales approach by discussing the five fundamental features of a successful sales assembly line operation.

SUMMARY OF THE GORILLA GAME

	Direct Sales	Inside Sales	Sales Assembly Line
Sales Professionals	4	4	4
Price of Product	$50,000	$50,000	$50,000
Appointments per Month	32	64	240
Appointments per Year	384	768	2,880
Close Rate	10%	8%	18%
Customers	38	61	518
YR 1 Gross Sales	1,900,000	3,050,000	25,900,000
YR 1 Costs of Sales	3,882,2000	2,076,000	5,598,000
YR 1 Net Sales Revenue	(1,982,000)	974,000	20,302,000
Company Expenses	12,940,000	6,920,000	18,660,000
Company Net Revenue	(11,280,000)	(3,870,000)	7,240,000
YR 2 Gross Sales	3,420,000	5,490,000	46,620,000
YR 2 Costs of Sales	4,064,400	2,368,800	6,118,000
YR 2 Net Sales Revenue	(644,400)	3,121,200	40,002,000
Company Expenses	13,548,000	7,896,000	22,060,000
Company Net Revenue	(10,128,000)	(2,406,000)	24,560,000
YR 3 Gross Sales	4,636,000	7,442,000	63,196,000
YR 3 Costs of Sales	4,210,320	2,603,000	6,618,000
YR 3 Net Revenue	425,680	4,838,960	56,578,000
Company Expenses	14,034,400	8,676,800	22,060,000
Company Net Revenue	(9,398,400)	(1,234,800)	41,136,000

Due to the incredible throughput of a Web-Meeting Sales Assembly Line, the platform is able to create and project a footprint that is many times larger than what could be accomplished by a Direct or Inside Sales seller. When this type of force projection is combined with the ability to dramatically improve the close rate, it has a powerful multiplier effect that generates outsized gains in revenue.

SALES ASSEMBLY LINE VERSUS DIRECT SELLER

SALES ASSEMBLY LINE SELLER VERSUS DIRECT SELLER

7.5x APPOINTMENTS

1.8x CLOSE RATE

13x CUSTOMER

13x GROSS REVENUE

WEB-MEETING SELLER VERSUS INSIDE SALES SELLER

3.7x APPOINTMENTS

22x CLOSE RATE

8.9x CUSTOMER

8.9x GROSS REVENUE

CHAPTER 5

Core Principles of a Sales Assembly Line

THE FIRST PART OF THIS book showed how difficult it is for a B2B technology seller to succeed. Innumerable forces are at work that are designed by the invisible hand of the market to ensure that most companies will, at best, struggle to meet expectations or, at worst, fail miserably. Making matters worse, if possible, is the fact that in a technology marketplace, only one company will eventually succeed. This Marketplace Gorilla will eventually obtain a lion's share of the revenue and profits derived from the product space.

Up to this point, companies had a limited solution set at their disposal when trying to hyperscale. There was hope that the technology-powered inside sales model would be the salvation. But its relatively low average close rate has not enabled sellers to conquer the mass market. Certainly, the most popular avenue for escape from this serious predicament is an "emperor's new clothes" solution, where a struggling company continues to raise institutional funds that mask the fact that it will never achieve profitability or, more important, become the market leader.

Sellers can take solace in the fact that the Internet has once again come to the rescue. Business-to-business sellers can build an assembly line based on web-meeting software that will fundamentally change the nature of the sales game. This distribution approach can have a dramatic impact on the fortunes of the seller. For the first time, most sellers can achieve profitability while still gaining the ability to hyperscale and dominate a given market, and as a result, become the undisputed Marketplace Gorilla. Moreover, due to efficiencies surrounding the sales process, a web-meeting sales assembly line seller can accomplish this goal without relying on huge amounts of outside funds.

With this basic understanding of why this sales approach is a preferable course of action when selling a technology solution, let's examine the specifics of how a sales assembly line operation works. It is important to stress that this approach is its own beast, and to be truly successful, it is not enough just to discard in-person meetings and replace them with online conversations. Instead, many of the fundamental truisms that make up the foundation of a traditional sales force must also be abandoned and replaced with new ideas on how a sales force should be structured. This section will discuss a number of operating principles which, if implemented correctly, should form the core of a successful sales assembly line operation.

1. THE USE OF FREE

Ever since Gillette gave away razors to sell razor blades or Jell-O gave away cookbooks to convince housewives to try gelatin, the concept of "free" has been a powerful business tool. In the Internet age, this strategy has spawned numerous successful companies such as Salesforce.com, Evernote, and Slack. Behavioral economists have examined why this simple four-letter word is so enticing to buyers. In study after study, at its most basic level, the word "free" elicits and stimulates an irrational emotional response that helps consumers ignore the potential downsides of an economic transaction. In addition to lowering the perceived risk, it also makes the buyer perceive what is being offered as immensely more valuable than it really is.

At first glance, it is easy to assume that "free" simply means free and equates to a business giving away a product or service without charge. However, this is an oversimplification. "Free" actually comes in many forms, including:

- **Direct Cross Subsidies.** A model where a seller gives away something free to a customer that will entice the potential buyer to pay for something else (e.g., buy one and get one free).

- **Freemium.** A model where a small number of paying customers subsidize nonpaying customers. This model is most often seen when companies widely release a stripped-down or trial version of the product or service and then charge a premium to a small number of other buyers.

- **Three-Party Markets.** A model where a third party subsidizes the sales of the product. A prime example of this is Google, where advertisers subsidize the search services offered to the market at large.

CrossBorder Solutions, throughout its history, used each of these approaches in some shape or form. For one product, the company gave away consulting services to get the software subscription dollars. For another product line, the company distributed a tool that performed a basic analysis for free and then sold customers an enhanced version that included more sophisticated functionality for a premium price. In the beginning, the use of "free" was nothing more than a marketing gimmick to try and generate interest in a fledgling product. However, once the sales assembly line began to be used extensively, it became a central tenet of the company's product and pricing philosophy.

The concept of "free" becomes turbocharged when used in conjunction with a sales assembly line. Because the costs per sale are so amazingly low, the throughput is so incredibly high, and the close rate is so impressive, a fully optimized assembly line should be able to generate significant operating margins. This translates to a situation where the company is able to better subsidize the sales effort with free promotions without negatively impacting the bottom line. Moreover, the promotions can be much more aggressive, which dramatically increases their likelihood of success and can be used as a long-term strategy instead of a short-term gimmick. For example, CrossBorder Solutions was able to take prospects and customers on trips to five-star resorts, on a quarterly basis, without making a discernible impact on the bottom line.

Another reason the assembly line sales approach and "free" are so complementary is because the methodology allows the seller to reach so many potential prospects. The promotion can be a catalyst that changes the underlying dynamics of the market and even disrupts revenue streams of other market participants. In the traditional sales environment, since the sales professionals are speaking to so few companies, the enterprise would have to spend a small fortune in marketing dollars to let market participants know about the promotion! This makes the "free" offer expensive. This is not the case in the sales assembly line environment. Due to the high number of customer touches, the sales development team is perfectly able to promote the offering to a wide segment of the market in the normal course of its daily operations without spending extra money promoting the promotion.

Finally, and perhaps most important, the use of "free" helps improve the close rate of the seller. No matter what techniques are employed, the lack of face-to-face contact makes buying via a web-meeting sales channel somewhat risky for a certain segment of the marketplace. Since "free" eliminates at least some of the perceived risk surrounding a transaction, it becomes possible for buying laggards to feel more comfortable with this sales approach.

2. THE IMPORTANCE OF IMAGE

In a traditional direct sales organization, image—defined for these purposes as how a sales prospect perceives the selling company—is a critical component to a successful sales process. In the direct sales realm, the sales professional who visits with the prospect becomes the public persona of the selling company. While it sounds incredibly shallow, the visual imagery presented by this employee can make or break a sale, as it has an enormous impact on the comfort level of the buyer.

Clearly, when selling via the sales assembly line approach, this type of visual imagery is noticeably absent. As a result, the opportunity to make an important and expected connection is lost. The question then becomes: How can an assembly line seller compensate for the impersonal nature of the environment? An earlier chapter described how CrossBorder Solutions used sales engineers to overcome this obstacle. However, to improve the close rate, imagery is still critically important to the sales process, but the way it impacts buyers has undergone a fundamental two-part shift.

The first shift happens when the buyer compensates for the absence by shifting focus from the salesperson to the selling company itself. In this light, the buyer will form the most salient impressions of the seller from the company's website and the marketing and sales-related materials that support the sales process. With this in mind, the image the company projects is critically important to the sales process. If a sales assembly line seller is going to be successful, the company must carefully manage its public face. It cannot look or act like a young, immature concern. Instead, the company should spend the necessary money to promote an image that projects stability and market leadership. Websites, marketing materials, email campaigns, and advertisements that look inexpensive will lower the close rate and likely irreparably harm the emerging company in the Early Majority market.

The second compensating shift occurs when the buyer focuses on how the sales professional sounds over the phone rather than how he or she looks in person. Auditory imagery helps the prospect conjure an image of the salesperson as an extension of the product itself. Therefore, how a sales professional sounds over the phone has a direct correlation to his or her selling success or failure.

A statistical analysis of this area showed that the most effective voice was devoid of an accent and spoke clearly, confidently, and concisely, almost as a news anchorman would sound. At CrossBorder Solutions, the company felt so strongly about auditory imagery that during any interview process the prospective sales professionals were taped and their voices were analyzed against what was considered the established ideal.

3. EMPLOYING MASS-PRODUCTION THEORY

Before the industrial revolution, "craftsman" production was the principal form of manufacturing. Under this approach, a single worker would be solely responsible for completing a product from start to finish. This type of manufacturing was relatively inefficient, as the craftsman could only manufacture a relatively small number of products at any given time.

At the turn of the twentieth century, it became clear that the craftsman's way of doing business was no longer going to be effective to meet growing demand. This situation was rectified when manufacturers began to implement assembly lines. Modern manufacturing relied upon (1) labor specialization, (2) statistics and artificial intelligence to determine best practices that would lead to higher throughput and close rates, (3) specialized tools that ensured that each line worker adhered to the identified best practices, and (4) specialized technology to automate and optimize the end-to-end manufacturing process. The adoption of these techniques ushered in the second industrial revolution and fostered an unprecedented and phenomenal increase in productivity and material wealth.

A parallel can be drawn between the craftsman form of production and the traditional sales approaches used by most B2B sellers today. Like the craftsman, the direct or inside sales professional is often responsible for a large portion of the sales process. As we have learned, this method of custom sales is not only expensive but also makes it practically impossible for the seller to conquer the mass market. The seller will simply not meet with and close enough prospects to hyperscale successfully.

As such, to compete successfully in this winner-takes-all environment, a seller must abandon the traditional methods of sales and adopt a radically new approach that will allow the company to mass-produce sales at a cost-effective price. The only way this can be done is to apply many of the same techniques that traditional manufacturers have relied upon to increase their volume, standardize their quality, and lower their production costs. Specifically, a sales assembly line seller must adopt sales specialization, ensure that best practices are repeated over and over again, and use technology to ensure compliance and to optimize the process. Each is discussed below.

Sales Specialization

In his 1776 treatise, *The Wealth of Nations*, Adam Smith observed the benefits of the division of labor. This principle became the cornerstone of mass production theory. Before that, the traditional craftsman typically undertook many tasks that were only tangentially related to his primary skill. For example, not only would a blacksmith produce the horseshoes, but he would also source the raw materials, design the product, initially meet with the customer, and haggle over price. After the sale was made, he would produce the shoe, possibly deliver it to the farmer, and even install the shoe on the horse. Clearly, all these tasks dramatically reduced his horseshoe-making effectiveness! Moreover, the overall cost to make and sell the product had to be much higher to take into account all the other functions he had to perform.

With the advent of the assembly line, manufacturers adopted the theory of labor specialization to lower the cost of production and to increase throughput. On an assembly line, each worker was normally assigned one specific task, which he or she would repeat over and over again. The key to making the line operate in a cost-effective manner was to ensure that the "right worker" was assigned to each task. The "right worker" would be the individual best suited to perform the activity from an ability and cost perspective. This meant that in almost all cases, it was not necessary to have a highly skilled, expensive expert working at every stage of the manufacturing process. Instead, many tasks could be completed by a less skilled and therefore less expensive laborer.

As we discussed in the "Generalist" model, a traditional sales professional would normally function in a similar manner as the traditional craftsman. He or she would not only be responsible for selling the product or service but also for handling most of the tasks surrounding the sale. Specifically, the Generalist would research potential leads, undertake localized marketing campaigns, cold-call prospects, prepare correspondence, conduct the sales call, and perform any necessary follow-ups to close the deal. In many cases, after making the sale, the professional would maintain the relationship with the new client by providing ongoing customer support in addition to taking responsibility for renewals and any upsell opportunities. Factoring in travel, it is no wonder that the traditional salesperson can handle so few leads and close such a small number of new prospects per year. In fact, it has been calculated that a direct sales Generalist will often spend only 12 percent of his or her time actually selling.

It is extremely inefficient and ineffective to have a good salesperson, a professional who is likely one of the organization's most scarce and valuable resources, do anything but sell. The amount of time a salesperson spends selling is the single and most important gating factor in determining the throughput or volume of sales that can be made. So to optimize the sales process, the concept of labor specialization should be applied to the sales operation. Specifically, each additional task the sales professional typically undertakes should be removed from his or her purview and given to a professional who is either better equipped to perform the task or is a less costly, more readily available resource. For example, it makes no economic sense for the salesperson to cold-call leads, as this can be done by a much more junior, less expensive employee.

The same specialization process should be completed over and over again for each task that has been removed. For example, in the case of a sales development representative, who has developed a special skill for calling prospects and convincing them to schedule an appointment, this professional should not research his or her own leads, as this would lower his or her overall throughput. Instead, the task of researching should be given to a relatively junior marketing professional who might be more proficient in data search. This task-winnowing exercise should continue until the sales process closely resembles an assembly line.

An optimized sales assembly line contains the following stages:

- Lead Management: Determines flow and quantity of leads necessary. Enters inbound leads and batches of raw prospects into the sales automation system.

    ◦ Outbound lead research: Identifies, sources, and tests leads purchased from third parties
    ◦ Social media research: Identifies potential leads and connects through social media

- Campaign Management: Determines how leads should be dealt with by sales development reps (SDRs)

- Sales Development: Responds to inbound leads and cold-calls outbound leads

- Account Executive: Moves leads through the sales funnel until they close or die

  - Sales engineer: Helps conduct appointments and develop solutions
  - Customer Success Group: Owns the client experience and handles renewals
  - Technical Support
  - Onboarding

- Business Development: Identifies and works upsell opportunities

The following description is the optimal breakdown of roles along a fictional sales assembly line, along with a brief description of each assembly line worker's principal tasks.

Marketing

Sales purists will immediately notice that marketing was given a role on the sales assembly line. Many traditional organizations have an artificial wall between marketing and sales. This separation is rooted in the fact that there is a natural tension between these two groups. Sales is always complaining that the leads marketing provides are not "sales-ready," and on the flip side, marketing does not believe the sales team follows up properly on the leads they are given. To optimize the sales operation, it is important that the two groups learn to work together seamlessly. The best way to do this is to integrate marketing into the sales process.

The following are some of the roles that should be played by professionals within the marketing group.

Lead Management: A lead database is the list of prospect names the seller uses to cold-call and schedule sales appointments. In a traditional sales organization, the lead database is given short shrift by everyone involved in the sales process, starting with the line professionals and up to and including sales management. This is somewhat surprising, since the health of this asset is one of the key factors in determining the success or failure of the overall sales organization.

Typically, a newly hired direct sales professional is given a territory that has an associated prospect list. In most cases, the provenance of the list is unknown, and it is viewed with a degree of suspicion. The task of maintaining the database often falls squarely on the shoulders of the individual salesperson, just as it did with the line of sales predecessors. Specifically, it is part of the job to add new prospects to the database, delete those that are inappropriate, and update the contained data so information on each lead is accurate. More often than not, this is not done in any scientific manner that ensures the long-term quality of the data. Instead, the lead database associated with a territory is maintained only to the extent that the current salesperson can find the relatively small number of leads necessary to achieve quota.

In a traditional manufacturing assembly line, one would never have the riveter go out and source his or her own supply of rivets. Instead, there would normally be a separate and distinct role for professionals who source the supplies necessary to keep the assembly line running smoothly. This should be the case in the web-meeting sales assembly line environment as well. Specifically, the lead management task should be removed from the purview of the individual sales development or sales professional and centralized under the authority of a specific individual. In an optimized environment, this professional should maintain the quantity and quality of the leads that will be distributed to the sales development representatives for use in outbound calling.

In regard to quantity, the lead database professional first and foremost needs to ensure that the database has enough prospects to support the organization's goals. The web-meeting sales assembly line is an extremely high-volume operation, and as such, the database needs to be much larger than a database in a direct or inside sales environment. Specifically, on average, a sales development representative needs to be given approximately 160 leads per week or eight thousand leads per year to be fully utilized. To generate this volume, the administrator must ensure that inbound leads are entered into the database in real time and that high-quality lists are purchased from outside vendors. In addition, original research might be undertaken, especially from social media sources, to identify new leads.

To ensure the quality of the database, the professional must first keep the database clean by removing duplicates. Second, to increase efficiency, every lead's information should be complete and accurate. A number of outside enterprises, such as ZoomInfo.com, provide this invaluable service. Third, the professional should test the quality of each lead source before its leads are widely distributed to the entire sales team. Typically, this is done by distributing a small sample of names to the sales development staff and comparing its close rate to the historical close rate achieved by other vendors. Finally, sellers that enjoy large markets often score or rate leads before they are distributed, which can improve the close rate.

Once the leads have been properly identified, this database professional must ensure that the leads are distributed to the sales development professionals in a manner that ensures statistical equality between each sales professional.

Campaign Management: Blindly cold-calling names, even if they are scored, will not ensure a high enough close rate. It is critical that the calling operation be structured around calling campaigns, which are defined as calls with a specific purpose. In addition to developing the marketing materials and content that support each campaign's persona, the campaign management professional would design and implement three different types of calling campaigns. The first would be comparison or A/B test campaigns, in which the sales development representatives follow A/B test scripts, discussing offers and other aspects of the sales process with prospects. The second would be marketing action campaigns that test the impact of different direct marketing actions, such as emails, direct mail, and even advertising campaigns with prospects. For the third type, marketing synchronization campaigns, sales development representatives call prospects immediately after they have received a marketing asset.

In addition to establishing each type of campaign, this professional must assign and distribute a batch of leads to be called. Most important, however, the marketing professional works with the sales leadership to establish the calling cadence that will be employed. Simply using a brute-force method, where the SDR calls the prospect over and over again, will likely not generate a positive result. Instead, outbound calls must be interspersed with voice mail messages and personalized emails that contain specific trigger points that grab the prospect's attention and pique their interest in the solution being sold. Below is a sample cadence that can be used for basic outbound calls:

Contact	1	2	3	4	5	6	7	8	9
Email	EM1			EM2			EM3	EM4	EM5
Call		C1	C2		C3	C4		C5	C6
VM			VM1			VM2			

To optimize the results, it obviously would be beneficial to develop specialized cadences for each instance of a calling campaign. Of course, it is always beneficial to A/B test each calling cadence to fine-tune the message going to the prospect. By customizing the cadence to match the prospect's persona, sellers can achieve dramatic increases in the close rate associated with each type of campaign.

Finally, tracking the results of each campaign is absolutely critical. It is important to calculate the overall reach rate, the positive reach rate, the negative reach rate, the callback rate, and of course the close rate of each campaign. With this information, the campaign manager will be in the position to determine how to employ similar campaigns in the future.

Appointment Generation. If the lead database is the foundation of the web-meeting sales platform, then appointment generation is the oil that keeps a sales assembly line operating smoothly and hopefully growing. The only way a seller can operate at an optimal level is to offload this task to a dedicated resource called a sales development representative. To this end, one of the most fundamental premises of a sales assembly line operation is the separation of the lead-generation function from the account executives. Only by separating these two roles can the organization hope to generate enough qualified leads to keep the sales professional operating at an optimal level.

In many organizations where the appointment-generation role has been separated from the sales function, the sales development group remains part of the sales group. While a great deal depends on the leadership of the two teams, this structure can often be less than optimal. By attaching the two groups together, there is a much higher likelihood that the sales group will negatively influence how the SDRs do their jobs. For example, it is not uncommon to see the sales professionals urge the callers only to schedule "good" appointments. As the callers cannot make this determination, this simply lowers the volume of opportunities unnecessarily. See chapter six for a full discussion of this topic.

The goal of any sales organization is to generate as many inbound leads as possible. An inbound lead is a prospect that has self-selected and contacted the seller for more information on the solution being sold. Since they are proactively reaching out, there is a much higher likelihood that they will seriously consider or even purchase the solution being sold. In fact, a study outlined in the article "The Art of Cold Calling and the Science of Contact Ratios" by Ken Krogue from Inside-Sales.com determined that inbound leads have a ten times higher close rate than leads generated through outbound calling. These are golden opportunities that must be handled with great care if the sales organization is to be successful.

Surprisingly, the same study found that most B2B sellers do not treat inbound leads with any sense of urgency. On average, it takes a seller at least two days to call back an inbound lead. Even more surprising was the fact that 20 percent of respondent companies never even attempted to follow up on an inbound opportunity. This is unfortunate. The longer the time frame between receiving the lead and responding to it, the lower the chance it will result in a closed opportunity. The same study showed that if a seller reaches out to an inbound lead within five minutes of receipt, the contact rate is one hundred times higher versus waiting even thirty minutes, and the chance of scheduling an appointment is twenty-one times more likely. This makes a great deal of sense because in today's fast-paced environment, where attention spans are fleeting at best, reaching someone who is thinking about the solution while they are thinking about it is certainly better than calling someone after they have moved on to more pressing matters. If that is not a powerful enough reason to call someone back quickly, consider this final fact: The study showed that the company that contacts the inbound lead first has an 80 percent higher chance of closing vis-à-vis other companies that are selling a comparable solution. Therefore, in an environment where most purchasers look at multiple solutions, reaching the buyer first is critical to sales success.

Based on this research, the system controlling the sales assembly line must ensure that inbound leads are reached, if at all possible, within the five-minute window. There are a number of ways to achieve this goal. One is to have the system automatically place the inbound lead in front of the next available outbound sales development representative, who would immediately call the inbound prospect within five minutes. Of course, if the inbound lead has dealt with a particular SDR or sales professional in the past, the system should route the lead to this professional. In cases where the volume of inbound leads is high, companies often have a separate team of SDRs that handle inbound leads exclusively.

While inbound leads are certainly ideal, most companies cannot generate enough of them to optimize the potential revenue opportunity. Therefore, outbound lead generation is an absolute necessity in most sales assembly line organizations. In an optimized environment, an outbound caller should be responsible for making over two hundred dials and generating three to four qualified appointments per day. This number assumes that the caller is using a system that *intelligently* selects the next prospect to call and is using a scientifically designed cadence. If the caller is picking and pecking through the pipeline, the number will drop to less than one hundred dials per day, with a corresponding decrease in appointments. The key to success in this role can be summed up in one word: persistence. The InsideSales.com study discussed above found that an outbound caller must make, on average, six dials per lead to optimize the number of appointments scheduled.

Lead generation or sales development specialists are primarily evaluated on the number of dials made, leads reached, appointments generated, and appointments that take place. Some organizations also compensate these professionals on the number and amount of deals closed, although this should not be a primary compensation driver, as it will skew the activities of the SDRs. It is debatable whether the sales development professional should confirm the appointment or if the sales professional should handle this task. Most companies have the sales professional confirm the meeting, so as to qualify the prospect more effectively. That being said, having the lead generation specialist remind the prospect with an email or phone call increases the possibility of the sales call occurring.

In most cases, the prospect being called by the sales development representative will not reach the lead on the first dial. In fact, it might take up to nine dials to reach the individual. Traditionally, companies simply would call and call again with the hope that the prospect would pick up. Recently, it has been determined that interspersing calls with emails and voice mail messages can increase the likelihood the prospect will eventually pick up the phone and schedule an appointment. Consequently, sophisticated outbound calling operations often provide their sales development teams with specific calling cadences to follow. For example, a caller might make four calls and leave three voice mails and two emails in a specific pattern. Naturally, different cadences should be used according to the type of campaign being undertaken. Moreover, it is important to A/B test the cadences to determine the optimal calling pattern.

Sales

Once leads are scheduled by the sales development team, they are passed off to the sales team. Lead distribution can occur through many different methods. Many companies, due to the limitations of their internal systems, pair sales development representatives with sales professionals called account executives (AEs). This often leads to less-than-optimal results, as this approach can penalize AEs who are not teamed with a competent SDR. The AE can also be hurt if a sales development representative leaves. Finally, and perhaps most important, teaming SDRs with AEs makes it difficult to preserve statistical equality between sales professionals, which interferes with management's ability to objectively compare performance results.

Alternatively, other operations use a round-robin approach,

which preserves statistical equality but makes it difficult to schedule appointments according to the needs of the prospect. The best approach is a more sophisticated solution that takes into account the needs of the prospect, but at the same time ensures that each sales professional receives the same number of appointments per month, thereby preserving statistical equality.

The sales group is responsible for converting these opportunities into sales. This group typically comprises three types of professionals.

Hunters. The Hunter is an AE who receives the opportunity from the sales development group. It is his or her job to qualify the opportunity, perform the initial appointment, run the opportunity through the sales funnel, and close as many deals as possible. In an optimized sales assembly line environment, the Hunter should expect to receive three appointments per day and be running approximately 120 to 150 deals at any given time, with the exact number based on average close rates and sales cycle. As this is a web-meeting sales environment, the Hunter will perform the first and any other appointments over the Internet, using web-meeting software. In this medium, it is best to keep all appointments to an hour or less if possible, as anything longer will cause the prospect to lose attention. When the Hunter is not engaging in first or follow-up online appointments, he or she should be spending most of the day following up with prospects over the phone and via email or social media. On average, the salesperson should have approximately twenty conversations per day with pipeline opportunities.

As in any sales environment, the principal way a Hunter should be evaluated is by his or her ability to meet a defined quota. When using a sales assembly line, it is often beneficial to use a monthly quota system rather than a quarterly or yearly system, as a monthly version better aligns with a high-volume operation and helps ensure that issues are identified in real time. However, there are other factors to consider. First and foremost is the salesperson's close rate, as defined by the ratio of closed sales to opportunities provided to the professional. This performance indicator gauges whether the sales professional is working every lead to its fullest extent and not cherry-picking, or even worse, "big-game" hunting. This is critical since the company likely spent a significant amount of money, time, and effort generating every single opportunity. Second, the sales professional's appointment-perform rate should be constantly monitored. A low percentage might mean the sales professional is "sandbagging" appointments. Not only will this result in lower overall sales, but it also wastes valuable resources. Finally, management should look at the second-demo perform rate, the deal-failure rate, the daily-conversation rate, and the amount of time each deal spends in each sales bucket.

Sales Engineers. In the sales assembly line environment, the sales engineer is a product or industry expert who can help build trust in the solution being offered. One of the benefits of web-meeting sales is that a sales engineer can cost effectively join any online meeting, which has been shown to raise the close rate significantly. This type of professional should join as many web meetings as possible and should also be considered when scheduling appointments. During the actual appointment, due to the sales engineer's industry and product experience, the best result is often achieved when the sales engineer conducts most of the meeting. This approach turns the conversation into a discussion rather than a sales call, which builds a great deal of comfort in the solution being sold. In these cases, the sales professional's role is typically limited to the introduction and the close. Of course, the sales engineer might also be responsible for crafting the solution and even drafting the proposal. When the sales engineer takes on these functions, the sales professional has more time to do what he or she does best—close deals! It is critical to track the close rates associated with each engineer, as this number is an indication of his or her level of sophistication and prowess.

Sales Assistants. If a salesperson is going to run more than one hundred deals per month successfully, there is apt to be a fair amount of written communication going back and forth with each individual prospect. To keep deals moving quickly, this communication must be accomplished in a timely manner. In the sales assembly line environment, where the prospect never meets with the seller face-to-face, the image associated with the selling company takes on even greater importance. This means the quality of any correspondence can play an outsize role in influencing the outcome of the sales process. Therefore, a professional whose full-time job is to handle these responsibilities is in a critical position in this environment.

Note, too, that sales professionals should not be allowed to hold prospects indefinitely, as this can clog their pipeline and make it difficult to find and focus on the "live" opportunities. Prospects that do not close in a reasonable amount of time should be returned to the lead database, where they will be recycled and called again by the sales development specialists. Depending on the reason behind the sales failure, campaigns can be established for targeting these leads with specialized offers down the road. In the sales assembly line environment, opportunities that close are handed off to the customer success team.

Customer Success

In many direct and inside sales situations, once a deal closes, the salesperson remains responsible for the client. While the salesperson might not provide actual technical support, he or she often retains ownership of the customer and is ultimately accountable for success or failure. In this type of situation, the sales professional typically is the client's liaison to the rest of the organization. Due to the continuing relationship, this professional would also handle any upsell and renewal opportunities.

In a direct sales structure, having the Generalist handle upsells and renewals makes sense. First and foremost, the post–sales relationship is built on a successful presale relationship, which should enable the seller to achieve a higher renewal rate and upsell additional products and services. Second, it helps prevent the salesperson from over-promising and underdelivering, as he or she will have to deal with the consequences personally. Third, if the customer is used to dealing face-to-face with the salesperson, it makes sense to continue this rela-tionship with the resource who is responsible for the territory where the customer is located.

While these reasons are valid, they hold less sway in a sales assembly line. For a number of important reasons, the customer success function should always be separate and apart from the sales function. Maintain-ing customer relationships is often time consuming. Spending time on existing clients will greatly detract from the number of new leads the sales professional can handle. In addition, a true Hunter, someone who is naturally aggressive, is often not the best person equipped to coddle and "cuddle" customers. Customer-success professionals are typically more junior and therefore less expensive than the sales professionals, so using them in these roles will improve operating margins.

Finally, and perhaps most important, as the sales truism goes, a sales professional will work the deals that will make him or her the most money. As new sales are normally harder to make than upsells and renewals, the Hunter salesperson should be compensated for these at a higher rate. In a combined environment, this will naturally cause the sales professional to spend more time and effort on new sales to the detriment of renewal sales. Therefore, often the only way to ensure that both renewals and upsells are properly handled is to pay the salesperson the same commission rate on renewals that they receive on new sales. This can become incredibly expensive and nega-tively impact the profitability of each customer. By splitting the sales roles, the seller can pay different commission rates while ensuring that each type of deal is appropriately worked.

One remaining issue is whether the customer success professionals should report to the sales group or if they should have their own separate reporting structure in the sales assembly line environment. As customer success should be staffed with specialized professionals who perform different tasks than the sales professionals, it makes a good deal of sense to separate the two groups. Even more important, completely separating the two revenue streams makes sense from a risk-management perspective. In this case, if the professional in charge of the sales group leaves, the revenue stream associated with renewals will not be impacted, and vice versa.

In the sales assembly line environment, the customer success function has a number of specialized roles that should ideally be performed by different professionals, including the following:

Customer Management. Once an opportunity becomes a client, it moves from the sales department into the customer success group, where it should be distributed to a customer management professional. Customer management professionals "own" the client in the organization and ensure that the client is successful. To accomplish this, customer management professionals play multiple roles. First, they typically are the liaison to the rest of the organization. Second, if it is an optional product and the renewal is not guaranteed, this professional should "cuddle" the customer by reaching out and speaking with the customer at regular intervals. How often the client is reached depends greatly on how automatic the renewal is for the seller. If a product has a low degree of stickiness, the client will need more hugs more often. Finally, the customer management professional should be responsible for managing the sales funnel the client will go through as they move through the renewal process together. In regard to the latter two roles, web meetings should be employed as often as possible, as they will help the professional develop the necessary relationship with the client.

In the average sales assembly line organization, customer management professionals normally handle 100 to 150 clients per year.

Typically, they are evaluated on key performance indicators, such as the number of dials, reaches, and conversations; close rates; and overall renewal rates. Compensation is based on these indicators and a quota system. Since renewals are easier to make than a new sale, base compensation and commission rates should be significantly less than what is paid to the sales professional.

Customer Support/Onboarding. Depending on the volume of clients, it often makes sense to hand off the customer support and onboarding function to an employee who is separate and apart from the customer management professional. This allows the latter to focus on building the overall client relationship and generating a healthy renewal rate. These professionals normally would be paid at a much lower rate and would not receive a commission on the renewal but might get a small bonus based on the company's overall renewal rate.

Business Development. When there are substantial upselling opportunities (e.g., product and service add-ons or new products), some sellers hire an employee who is a hybrid between a sales and a customer management professional. This person should be less aggressive than the typical Hunter but more aggressive than the customer management professional, who needs to maintain a positive relationship to secure the renewal. As with the account executives, web meetings and sales engineers should be used to improve the throughput of the team as well as its close rate. As this is an in-between position, these professionals are often paid more than customer success professionals but less than the Hunter salesperson.

Sales Operations

The sales assembly line is an operation with many moving parts. Adding to its complexity is the fact that it spans many different divisions, each with their own goals and priorities, within the organization. While the CEO's involvement is critical to the successful implementation of the approach, it is unlikely that he or she has the time to ensure that the operation is optimized daily. Similarly, although the active involvement of the VP of sales, VP of customer success, and VP of marketing is similarly important, placing the day-to-day responsibility of how the assembly line functions in their purview is discouraged, due to interdepartmental rivalries and an overall lack of bandwidth. To solve this dilemma, many enterprises rely on a director of sales operations. This professional works closely with all the stakeholders to drive sales results.

The key to operating a successful, high-velocity sales assembly line is to continually examine and streamline each sales process. This is especially the case as the team scales to meet the growing demand that is a hallmark of this sales approach. Typically reporting to the CEO or VP of sales, the director of sales operations is the glue that holds the assembly line together. While developing the processes that make the line über-efficient is certainly important, a big part of this job is to carefully examine and interpret the data that the line continually generates to ensure it is operating in an optimal manner. Typically, another responsibility is to train the team in the various processes and to make sure each team member is complying with the established standards.

Additional Benefits of Sales Specialization

Sales specialization can provide a web-meeting sales assembly line seller with other benefits.

- Traditionalists often argue that having specialized resources lowers performance because the specialist will be less skilled than the salesperson, who is the most senior person on the assembly line. This is not the case. As these other resources are spending 100 percent of their time focusing on their specific tasks, they quickly become über "experts."

- When any professional engages in more than one task, it becomes difficult to evaluate the individual's performance accurately. This is because it gets substantially harder to establish reliable internal benchmarks and then to compare professionals against one another. For example, take the traditional sales professional who handles lead generation and new sales. In this situation, it would be difficult for management to determine whether the professional is making an optimal number of cold calls. If the number is low, does this indicate laziness or does it mean that compared to coworkers, this person has more sales opportunities and does not need to add anything to his or her pipeline? Compare this to the situation where a SDR does nothing but cold-call all day. In this case, it is easy to establish an optimal number.

- Successful sales professionals are constantly being poached by other organizations. One of the best ways to prevent this is to make the work environment as pleasant as possible so employees do not want to leave. One way to do this is to remove the tasks they hate from their responsibilities. For example, cold-calling is generally one of the most unpleasant aspects of a salesperson's job description. Removing this task will likely dramatically increase job satisfaction, which will boost retention and even make it easier to attract high-quality sales professionals. At CrossBorder Solutions, when sales candidates were told they no longer had to make cold calls and instead would be presented with hundreds of qualified leads per year, it was not difficult to convince them to join and stay with the company.

- The aforementioned structure also provides a pathway for professional development. Typically, the most obvious route to becoming a sales professional is to move from sales development to sales. At CrossBorder Solutions, this route often did not work well. Sales development professionals are typically too junior to be successful in the Hunter role, especially for a sophisticated product. Numerous times I have seen a great SDR promoted to sales and then fail miserably and wind up leaving the company. This is a tremendous waste of a valuable resource. A better approach is to have the sales development representative graduate to become a customer management professional. Customer management professionals who have experience closing renewal business can graduate to business development, where they learn to close new business in a more forgiving environment. Finally, with this experience, successful business development professionals are perfectly suited to move into the Hunter position.

By aligning the skills of the professionals with the different tasks in the sales process, a sales assembly line seller can become dramatically more productive. In fact, with this breakdown of roles, the seller's assembly line will be in the position to handle up to seven times the number of leads compared to a traditional sales operation. Moreover, the operation itself will become much more profitable, as the seller is able to have less expensive resources performing the tasks associated with making the sale and ensuring customer success.

Traditional CRM software products were designed for the Direct Seller who travels to the prospect's work site and deals with a relatively low volume of sales. These packages do NOT allow the web-meeting seller to efficiently and effectively manage a high velocity sales assembly line.

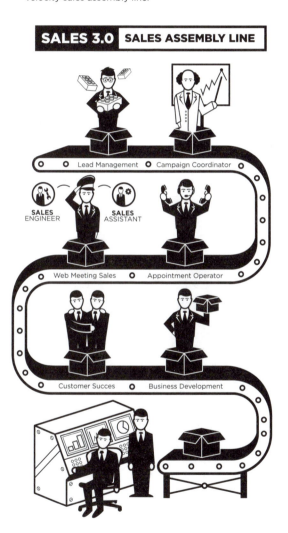

SALES 3.0 **SALES ASSEMBLY LINE**

Lead Management   Campaign Coordinator

SALES ENGINEER   SALES ASSISTANT

Web Meeting Sales   Appointment Operator

Customer Succes   Business Development

ADVANTAGES

Increased Sales Throughput

Lower Costs of Sales

Improvement of Close Rate Through Specialization

Improved Ability to Evaluate Performance

Happier and More Productive Sales Force

Discovery of Repeatable, Best Practices

Assembly lines would not work effectively if production decisions were left to the individual workers. Consider what would happen on a traditional manufacturing assembly line if each worker were allowed to perform a task as he or she saw fit. While many products might be produced, it is highly likely that each product would be slightly different and the quality would be uneven at best. Therefore, one of the hallmarks of a traditional manufacturing assembly line is that it produces the same exact product over and over again. When it is working properly there should be no discernible difference between each item coming off the line.

To operate properly, every action along the line must be centrally planned, tightly controlled, and above all else, repeatable over and over again. To be successful, every step in the manufacturing process must be determined in the utmost detail so a series of best practices are developed. Then, the line must be constantly monitored to ensure that every repeatable action is being followed to the exact specifications. Not only does this ensure a consistent result, but the massive data sets generated from the processes can be mathematically analyzed so the results can continually be used to refine and continually improve the assembly line's overall operating performance.

Specifically, the first step is to centrally plan the sales manufacturing process from start to finish. This exercise starts with creating a sales map. This is a diagram of each and every function undertaken by the organization when making a new or renewal sale. To optimize the process, each primary function must be broken down into individual tasks in excruciating detail. It is critical that every action, no matter how seemingly small, is identified and dissected.

Once the sales map has been developed, it is necessary to figure out how to optimize each task. Remember that most existing methods have been developed through a fundamentally flawed trial-and-error process that has likely impacted the seller's ability to survive. If these same outdated practices are followed in the sales assembly line environment, the company will forfeit many of the benefits associated with specialization and will also achieve a less than optimal close rate. Therefore, to successfully hyperscale, a high-velocity sales assembly line must find a way to identify the best practices for each task.

While many of these decisions can be made by multidisciplinary teams that carefully examine and weigh different approaches, in some cases it will be necessary to scientifically determine the right approach. Whether using third-party data, A/B tests, or other forms of statistical analysis, the seller's goal is to develop a series of processes that lead to a higher level of throughput or close rate. This work plan will become the North Star for the team as it prepares to implement the sales assembly line.

The decision to adopt a new sales approach is not an easy one. It is natural to feel apprehensive about moving away from a well-trodden, conventional strategy—even one that almost guarantees that the company will eventually fail. While the effort can certainly be designed and spearheaded by the VP of sales or VP of marketing, a decision this important demands the direct involvement of the CEO, who will need to be the main force behind the transformation. Since the sales assembly line spans so many in-house departments, without strong leadership, it is doubtful that the entire organization will have the courage and internal fortitude to make this type of change. In my experience, in situations where the CEO has not been an active participant in moving the entire company in the same direction, the end result has been less than optimal.

Tools to Ensure Compliance with Best Practices

In the sales environment, it can be difficult to convince the professionals on the line to follow the established procedures, as they are accustomed to having a great deal of leeway on how they deal with their daily responsibilities. However, if systems are not put into place to ensure actions are repeatable and strictly followed, the entire effort of figuring out what works and what doesn't will have been for naught. There are a number of ways this can be accomplished in the sales assembly line environment, including the following:

- The brute-force method, in which management exerts influence over the staff. In this light, many companies have hired a director of sales operations, whose role is to oversee the staff and ensure they are complying with established procedures. In our experience, while this can be helpful, the "Big Brother" aspect of it can sometimes impede compliance.

- If the system controlling the sales assembly line can generate both real-time and historical performance data and share it with each professional, this can positively influence behavior without being overbearing. The gamification of this sharing process with leader boards, internal contests, and so on, can certainly encourage sales professionals to comply with the established best practices.

However, the best way to make the processes repeatable is to provide the professionals with specialized tools that enable them to easily perform the tasks under their purview. In a perfect world, these tools will have been customized for each action, which eliminates the friction that often impedes compliance. In this light, it is extremely important to provide tools that *only* allow individuals to undertake the prescribed activity. All too often, in trying to be something for everyone, sales automation systems provide an endless menu of choices. Having a myriad of choices is a prescription for the professional to stray from established procedures.

Specialized Technology to Manage and Optimize the Assembly Line Operation

In the days when a single craftsman manufactured a product, he needed only a relatively unsophisticated tool set to be successful. This ceases to be the case in an assembly line environment. Not only does each worker need specialized tools to perform their repetitive task easily, but systems must be in place that constantly evaluate the performance of every aspect of the process so it can undergo a cycle of improvement. In addition, with a high volume of product being produced across a number of stages, specialized technology helps to ensure the product moves from step to step efficiently and effectively.

The same holds true in a sales assembly line environment. In a traditional sales environment, most sales professionals rely on CRM software that was developed for the traveling Generalist. Such systems often suffer from many shortcomings when they are employed in a sales assembly line environment:

- They are complex and often difficult to use because they are developed to support a single professional's ability to handle a myriad of sales-related tasks.

- They do not handle large volumes of sales assets (leads, prospects, opportunities, customers) efficiently.

- They do not tightly structure the sales process, because they support the concept of providing the sales professional with a great deal of freedom on how to handle each sales asset.

- They collect information via a free-form process, which limits the system's ability to statistically analyze the data.

- They are territory based, which prevents equalization of assets.

- They do not seamlessly support sales specialization, so moving sales assets from one stage to the next is not seamless or easy to accomplish.

To try and counteract the above deficiencies, numerous third-party sales automation applications have been developed that sit on top of the basic CRM system. However, because the underlying foundation is so inappropriate for high-velocity sales methodologies, the resulting sales stacks are expensive and difficult to implement, maintain, and use. Therefore, to optimize a sales assembly line, sellers must use specialized technology designed to support the unique characteristics of this sales approach. In general, it is important that any system has the following attributes:

Sales Asset Flow Control. Any system must ensure that the human capital on the assembly line is efficiently employed. As such, the system must carefully calibrate the flow of sales assets to each professional to ascertain that they are dealing with the optimal number at any given time. For example, if a sales professional has too many opportunities, then he or she will not keep up and will likely cherry-pick, which will lower the overall close rate. Alternatively, if the professionals are presented with too few leads, they will be underproductive. Making this task more difficult is the fact that the system must calculate the optimal flow so every station is working in equilibrium with one another.

Raw Material Planning. For the assembly line to function, there must be a constant, steady supply of the materials needed to produce a sale. Specifically, taking into account production volume and timing, management needs to determine how many leads are necessary to introduce into the system on a daily basis. Similarly, it is critical to understand how many references the sales professionals will need to maintain the targeted close rate.

Randomization/Equalization. Continuous process improvement is a hallmark of any sales assembly line system. To accomplish improvement scientifically, it is absolutely critical to distribute sales assets to each professional on the line in a randomized but equal manner. If sales assets are not equal, it is impossible to compare the performance of each person and of the line itself.

Timing. How long a sales asset stays at each node of the assembly line and how much time the individual workers have to complete their respective tasks are critical factors that the system controlling the line must take into account. Otherwise, bottlenecks can occur that dramatically decrease the efficiency of the sales process. For instance, if it takes on average two minutes to process a cold call, the line must automatically make sure the SDR does not receive more than thirty leads per hour.

Role-Specific Functionality. Since sales specialization is so important, any system must support this concept and ensure that each worker on the line has specialized software that allows them to accomplish their task in an efficient and effective manner while collecting a wide range of performance data.

When CrossBorder Solutions was building out its assembly line, it attempted to use one of the leading commercial CRM packages. However, the system simply could not support sales specialization and therefore the company's goals. As a result, the company built its own sales assembly software that controlled every step of the sales and customer service process. This sophisticated piece of software was the underlying driver of the company's success. Many of the firms I have worked with since then have been forced to take this approach as well, to counteract the underlying deficiencies found in most CRM systems today. At CrossBorder Solutions, our system included the following features that allowed the company to optimize its sales assembly line operation:

Cognitive Circulation

The system seamlessly supported the concept of labor specialization and allowed multiple professionals to work in conjunction with one another to mass produce sales. To accomplish this, the system addressed three concepts:

1. The sales asset (lead, prospect, opportunity, customer) should automatically move from one stage to the next based on the input of the professional at each stop along the journey. Often, this is not a one-way, forward-looking path. For example, if a sales development representative sets up an appointment for the sales professional but the appointment does not occur, the lead needs to be sent back to the sales development representative to reschedule the meeting.

2. The system must calculate the flow of sales assets between each stage and ensure that the quantity and timing parameters are properly optimized to eliminate bottlenecks.

3. As the sales asset transitions from function to function, the software needs to distribute the lead to the right professional automatically and intelligently. This becomes more difficult when territories are no longer the deciding factor controlling distribution. Moreover, any distribution mechanism must maintain statistical equality, otherwise any measure of objective evaluation is circumspect.

4. The software should provide each person involved in the sales process with specialized views and tools to help them accomplish specific tasks. In many cases, professionals will play multiple roles, so the software must handle this as well.

Cognitive Calling

In a traditional environment, when cold-calling, a salesperson is estimated to spend 40 percent of his or her time trying to figure out whom to call next. This pick-and-peck method of selection is extremely inefficient from a number of perspectives. It wastes valuable time that should be used calling other leads. Also, in high-volume environments, it is extremely easy to experience system leakage where valuable opportunities slip through the cracks. Finally, providing sales development professionals with the ability to self-select the calls almost guarantees that their own internal biases will dictate their calling patterns rather than what might be optimal. For example, companies that are not well known often get ignored, while brand-name companies get called many times.

In an optimized web-meeting sales assembly line, where each professional along the sales assembly line is dealing with a deep, fast-moving river of leads constantly flowing through, the user of a typical CRM system will quickly become overwhelmed and underproductive. To rectify this situation, our system took the potential volume of leads into account when designing its interface for users. Instead of having sales development representatives select who to call, the sales system used sophisticated algorithms to decide who should be called, when they should be called, how often they should be called, and, based on the purpose of the call, how the call should be handled.

Cognitive Calendar

In a traditional sales environment, with the relatively low volume of sales, it is not difficult to schedule appointments. This is especially the case when the salespeople schedule their own meetings or when a typical sales development representative is scheduling an appointment for one salesperson in a defined territory. There are plenty of calendar systems that can handle this task with ease, and most CRM systems include this basic functionality.

However, in a high-velocity sales assembly line environment, potentially hundreds or even thousands of appointments are booked on a monthly basis. Scheduling becomes even harder when there are multiple different demo types, multiple resources, such as sales engineers, participating in the appointments, and the meetings are being scheduled in a manner to ensure statistical equality. Finally, the user of the calendar must find an open appointment slot quickly, before the prospect can reconsider and decide not to schedule an appointment. A streamlined calendar solution is critical.

CrossBorder Solutions' sales assembly line software system had an integrated calendar feature that helped the user quickly and efficiently find an "open slot" for a meeting with a prospect while taking into account all the parameters that needed to be considered. It also automatically used the optimal distribution algorithm so the "right" salesperson (i.e., the professional who needs the most demonstrations for the time period) was automatically scheduled for the appointment.

Cognitive Call Processing

With traditional CRM software, the user dealing with a lead, an opportunity, or a customer has a great deal of flexibility regarding how to handle the prospect interaction and then regarding what information to enter into the system documenting what has occurred. Typically, at a bare minimum, the sales professional will enter notes on each conversation, and if there is a next step, such as a future phone call or appointment, establish a "pending action." This information is stored so that the *individual* sales professional can understand where the situation stands and what needs to be done next.

This "flexible" data entry approach, however, makes it difficult, if not impossible, for anyone but the sales professional to track what has occurred with a prospective opportunity or client. This means that the sales-related data cannot be aggregated and analyzed, which prevents any statistical analysis of the information. This, in turn, makes it impossible to discover what is working, what is not, and what should be done to optimize the sales process. Moreover, there is no way to ensure that the sales professional is undertaking the optimal action based on the facts and circumstances surrounding the customer interaction. This basic structure only makes sense with the Generalist sales model, which assumes the salesperson is fully responsible for everything that occurs with the prospect.

This unstructured data approach also makes it difficult for the salesperson to work with opportunities in the most efficient manner possible. Often, in the course of a busy day, data is mistakenly omitted or is incomplete. In an environment where there are relatively few leads, it is easy for the sales professional to catch up. But in a high-velocity sales environment, where hundreds of leads are quickly moving in and out of a salesperson's queue on a monthly basis, it is likely that data will not be entered properly, and this will introduce inefficiencies into the line's operation and lead to missed opportunities.

To make sure the assembly line worked smoothly and efficiently at CrossBorder Solutions, the sales system incorporated a complex, self-reporting mechanism. Each station along the assembly line had a performance-monitoring feature, and a wide range of sales data at every step of the process was automatically collected. The system trapped two types of data. First, it collected system-level data that showed how well the assembly line was functioning in real time. For example, the system captured and aggregated how many appointments had been made, and the close rate by sales professional, product, and time period. Second, the system enabled the professional to "process" every interaction (positive or negative) with every sales asset. This allowed the system to capture the "right" information on each and every task undertaken by each professional along the line on a real-time basis. Moreover, the system forced the line professional to enter data in a standardized format so it could be aggregated and analyzed.

While capturing the data was important, it was critical that the information was reported clearly so the various stakeholders could objectively understand where things stood and how they could be improved. Our system processed the data and produced a wide range of management reports on each task along the sales assembly line. These reports were provided to all the stakeholders on a daily, weekly, and monthly basis. Moreover, when the company was in the process of being sold, these documents formed a basis of the overview of our operations. Our team's ability to provide this information in real time gave the potential buyers confidence in our numbers, which definitely increased our valuation.

Cognitive Campaigns

A disconnect between sales and marketing often exists in the traditional sales environment. Our system, however, integrated marketing into the sales automation process, to assist the sales assembly line seller in optimizing inbound and outbound lead generation. Our system allowed the marketing team to (1) manage the lead database, (2) establish calling campaigns to test the quality of lead lists, (3) coordinate fair and equitable lead distribution to appointment generators, (4) ensure that appointment generators received and processed inbound leads in real time, (5) establish calling campaigns to A/B test the messaging and other promotions, and (6) establish calling campaigns to follow up on outbound marketing activities.

Cognitive Course of Action

Through A/B testing and the evaluation of a wide range of statistics/ KPIs, it is now possible to determine what factors positively influence the close rate of the seller. Unless this information is used to develop best practices and ensure that the line professionals are following these guidelines, the collection of the data is for naught. Our system allowed management to establish customized instruction sets, or "plays," on how to deal with each type of prospect. For example, at CrossBorder Solutions, our internal sales automation system forced our account executives to follow a defined five-stage work flow that was proven to move the opportunity through the sales process in an optimized manner. Moreover, the system carefully tracked the results of each interaction so each play could be continuously evaluated and modified to fit changing circumstances. Ensuring that best practices were implemented and followed dramatically improved the close rate of the team.

Cognitive Casting

In a traditional sales environment, a salesperson will typically meet with his or her manager on a weekly or monthly basis to review the status of each prospect in the pipeline. In this meeting the sales professional will describe what has been done to move the prospect through the sales funnel and will provide the manager with an estimated closing price and even try to predict the probability of closing within a certain time frame. The manager takes this type of information from each salesperson, rolls it up, and then makes a team-wide sales forecast. Since everyone involved in this process is working off incomplete information and a healthy dose of guesswork, it is no wonder that sales forecasts are regularly missed by significant amounts. The absence of accurate forecasting negatively impacts the company in myriad ways.

While these meetings were important in our own sales assembly line environment, we didn't rely on them to provide forecasts. Instead, the sales system was responsible for establishing an accurate forecast. The software was able to calculate historical close rates for each lead in each sales bucket and then mathematically predict a monthly, quarterly, and yearly number. Over the years we employed this approach, it was exceedingly rare for the computed forecast not to match reality. This gave us a high degree of confidence when making financial decisions and reduced the financial surprises that young companies often encounter.

The foundation of our success was our internal software system and its ability to incorporate the sales assembly line methodology. The company never would have been able to achieve what it did without this solution.

WINNING THE

To dramatically improve sales throughput and to lower the direct costs of sales, a Web-Meeting Seller should construct a high-velocity sales assembly line.

USE OF TECHNOLOGY TO IMPROVE EFFICIENCY OF SALES ASSEMBLY LINE

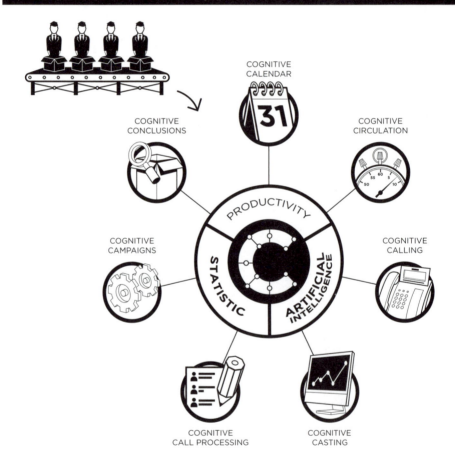

4. THE ELIMINATION OF TERRITORIES

The most basic and fundamental building block of an old-fashioned direct sales operation is the division of the marketplace into distinct, geographic territories. Territories are extremely useful when a salesperson must visit with prospects to close a sale. Allocating territories minimizes the amount of travel they need to undertake, which makes meeting prospects face-to-face more cost effective and time efficient. Sales territories can also help prevent collisions—the damaging situation where two different salespeople work on the same account simultaneously. Finally, having customers concentrated in a limited geographic area should help a sales professional successfully sell to prospects, as positive interactions between potential buyers will likely exist.

When selling via a sales assembly line, since the salesperson is no longer traveling to the prospect site, territories immediately become unnecessary and even harmful. Instead, a marketplace should be viewed as a single defined sales unit if the process is going to be fully optimized. This section will discuss how eliminating territories can become a powerful weapon in a seller's arsenal when attempting to improve close rates and conquer the mass market.

Improved Equalization of Opportunities

No matter how hard sellers try, it is next to impossible to ensure that territories are equal to one another. This impacts the organization from two different perspectives. First, from management's viewpoint, it makes it difficult to establish a consistent quota plan, properly evaluate talent, and generate reliable forecasts. It also increases the chance that good sales professionals will fail because of a bad territory while bad sales professionals succeed not because of their inherent skill set but simply because the territory is fertile. This does not optimize sales results.

For the sales professionals, unequal territories are also a constant source of frustration, as these employees are typically evaluated by how well they perform in a given geographic region vis-à-vis other sales professionals operating in different regions. To this end, it is not unusual for a sales organization to rank its salespeople based on their achievement of quota. The results of this comparison process often impact compensation, performance evaluations, promotions, and even future job opportunities with different employers. As it is important for a sales professional to do well compared to his or her peers, anything that artificially skews these results can sap morale, decrease job satisfaction, and hurt overall sales performance.

This inequality problem is taken off the table once territories have been eliminated from the mix. Instead of sourcing leads using a geographic arbitrator, in a sales assembly line environment the leads can be randomly distributed to each sales professional. This guarantees that everyone is operating on an even playing field and has the same opportunities to succeed or fail, which should result in a happier, more productive sales force.

Even more important, it allows management to compare the actions and results of each sales professional against the rest of the team *objectively*. For example, if Salesperson A, B, C, and D are receiving the same number of leads, and these leads are distributed on a randomized round-robin basis, it should be relatively easy to compare each professional's ability to close deals. If Salesperson A has a close rate of 22 percent while Salespeople B, C, and D have close rates of 24 percent, 19 percent, and 8 percent, respectively, it is clear that D is not making the grade and should perhaps be replaced, as he or she is simply wasting valuable opportunities.

Optimized Lead Distribution

To maximize sales, it stands to reason that the sales force should concentrate its efforts on prospects that are most apt to close. Territories often constrain the seller's ability to effectively concentrate on such prospects. For example, a seller may determine that software companies are purchasing its product at twice the rate of other buyer segments. Therefore, the seller would prefer to concentrate on this segment of potential buyers. However, having territories prevents the seller from taking full advantage of this opportunity. This is because the sales force is broken up into five geographic areas (Northeast, Southeast, Mid-Atlantic, Southwest, and Northwest), with one salesperson operating within each region.

In this example, the targeted software companies are not evenly spread out among these territories. Not surprisingly, there is a dramatically higher concentration of targets in the Northeast and Northwest, which means the salespeople operating in these two territories have more leads than they can effectively handle, and that business is being left on the table for competitors to pick up. Conversely, salespeople operating in the other geographic areas have a paucity of strong software leads and are not able to take advantage of the market opportunity.

Contrast the above situation to an assembly line seller who does not rely on territories. Upon discovering the affinity that software companies have for the products, the seller would simply create a calling campaign and distribute all the software company leads in the United States equally among the five sales professionals. This would optimize the opportunity. This type of distribution pattern can become a true competitive advantage because it allows the web-meeting seller to overwhelm competitors quickly in specific industries, as he or she can operate across territorial boundaries.

Integrating Additions to the Sales Teams

When geographic territories are used, it can be difficult to accommodate additions to the sales force. Adding a salesperson to an existing territory necessitates taking away potential prospects from an existing salesperson. Even if the territory can support an additional resource, the existing sales professional will have fewer leads to work with, which will certainly negatively impact his or her ability to cherry-pick opportunities. This can be disruptive to morale, as it negatively impacts the ability of the existing sales professionals to earn.

Once again, an assembly line seller who is operating without territories will not be faced with this issue. When a new salesperson is hired, the distribution algorithm is simply changed to reflect the addition of the new professional. Assuming there is not a paucity of leads, this addition will barely be noticed, as the impact is spread among the entire team.

Effective Revenue Rescue

A similar situation occurs in revenue rescue scenarios. Typically, when a sales professional who is assigned to a territory leaves the employ of the seller, the territory stops being worked until a new salesperson is hired. In the short term, in an attempt to rescue revenue immediately, management will typically pass "live" leads to existing professionals to try and save deals. For a number of reasons, this approach tends to be unsuccessful in a territory-based company.

Unless there are other sales professionals working in the territory, it is difficult, if not impossible, for someone else to jump in and cover a new geographic area. Even if they have the available bandwidth to deal with the new opportunities, it is likely that the sales professional will cherry-pick the leads and only "run" those with a chance of closing in the immediate short term. The covering salesperson fully realizes that when someone new is hired, the leads are going to be given back to the new professional in order to maintain the region's integrity. This is a particularly serious issue, considering the fact that the average sales force experiences 20 percent to 30 percent turnover per year.

Eliminating territories can dramatically improve the effectiveness of the revenue rescue efforts. Since there is no territory to preserve, existing leads owned by a departing sales professional can be intelligently and *permanently* reallocated among the existing sales staff. This dramatically increases the chance they will be fully worked, especially if the sales automation system is programmed to ensure this result.

Territory Ownership

One of the by-products of a geographic, territory-based sales organization is that typically the sales professionals operating within the territory "own" the space. This often means that the sales professional is responsible for everything that occurs with prospects—and even sometimes customers—in the defined market area. As a result, the salesperson normally wants absolute control, or close to it, over everything that might impact his or her ability to generate income. The practical impact of this is twofold. First, the sales professionals will often find themselves handling non-sales-related tasks, which can dramatically reduce the sales professional's throughput and increase the sales operation's expense. Second, in this environment, the salesperson is right to demand—and management should agree within reason—the necessary freedom from micromanagement of the sales process.

We previously espoused the benefits of pursuing an inclusive approach to sales management. Eliminating territories gives the team the vehicle to accomplish this in an efficient manner. In the absence of territories, the various sales assets (e.g., leads, prospects, opportunities, and customers) become the undisputed property of the company, rather than the individual salesperson. This expanded outlook can help the team optimize how each interaction is handled with every prospect and client.

In the sales assembly line environment, the best way to influence behavior is to manipulate the allocation of leads, which is almost impossible to do in a territory-based environment. For example, professionals who perform actions correctly might get additional leads from the sales system, which should result in more income. Similarly, compliance with sales processes can be encouraged through bonuses or even participation in special events such as President Club trips.

ELIMINATION OF TERRITORIES
in a Sales Assembly Line Environment

TRADITIONAL SALES STRUCTURE

SALES TERRITORIES

CENTRAL TERRITORY

NORTHEASTERN TERRITORY

EASTERN TERRITORY

WESTERN TERRITORY

SOUTHWESTERN TERRITORY

SOUTHERN TERRITORY

- Prevents Collisions
- Minimizes Travel
- Improves Close Rate
- Lowers Cost of Sales

SALES ASSEMBLY LINE STRUCTURE

WEB-MEETING SALES ENVIRONMENT

When selling via a web-meeting sales force, territories are completely unnecessary and even harmful. Instead, a marketplace should be viewed as a single defined sales unit to better optimize the sales process.

ELIMINATION OF TERRITORIES BENEFITS

SALES PERSON	EFFECTIVE PERFORMANCE COMPARISON			EFFICIENT REVENUE RECOVERY				EFFECTIVE ON-BOARDING			
	A	B	C	A	B	C	D	A	B	C	D
DEMOS	25	25	25	24	24	24	24	24	24	24	
CLOSED DEALS	10	12	18	32	32	32	0	24	24	24	24

5. USING STATISTICS TO EVALUATE AND INFLUENCE SALES BEHAVIOR

In the book *Moneyball*, Michael Lewis describes how using sabermetrics changed the management of Major League Baseball. The book describes in detail how the perennially losing Oakland A's were consistently able to surpass "big money" teams and become one of the best teams in baseball. They became better able to compete by applying a wide range of statistical techniques to determine mathematically whom to draft, who should play, and even what to do in specific game situations. These tools replaced the ubiquitous "gut call" that had been a staple of baseball decision making.

The publication of *Moneyball* ushered in a period of heightened interest in how statistics could be used by a wide range of businesses to optimize their performance. The ability to analyze big data statistically is now a standard management technique for decision makers who are looking for a competitive advantage. Over the past few years, data-driven decision making has begun to make inroads at the edges of the sales department.

Most sales operations, however, have found it difficult to use statistics effectively and widely. It is enormously challenging to account for standard deviations in the data when territories are employed and when sales professionals undertake many roles. Also, most CRM systems do not systematically capture the information necessary for this type of analysis. Another hindrance is the relatively small number of impressions generated by a traditional business seller. Probably the largest stumbling block to widespread adoption is the individualistic nature of sales: Many participants still believe that sales is an "art" that does not lend itself to mathematical introspection.

Failing to embrace statistics as a management technique in the sales department has been shown to have a negative impact on performance and revenue. While the "traditional" experts are long on experience, study after study has proven that the "gut call" decision-making process is fundamentally flawed. Even though experts strenuously claim that crunching data cannot capture the expertise gained over a lifetime of experience, in a complex sales organization, the mental wherewithal to see the forest instead of the trees simply does not exist, as there are too many variables to consider. In this regard, sales managers cannot make predictions with any degree of accuracy. This leads sales managers to make incorrect and inaccurate calls constantly on everything from staffing levels to forecasting.

The web-meeting sales assembly line approach dramatically improves the chances to use and rely on statistics to make more accurate predictions. Specialization of roles, structured sales processes, the elimination of territories, and above all, the relatively large number of impressions all mean that statistical number crunching can become significantly more reliable. In the sales assembly line environment, three types of statistical analyses can be employed.

Professional Evaluation Statistics

In a traditional sales environment, it is difficult to effectively compare sales professionals to one another. Not only does this make it hard to figure out who is good and who is bad, but it also prevents the seller from determining what factors in the sales process impact this determination. Traditional sellers understand this limitation and rely on straight quota as a comparison tool, despite the fact that this number often provides an incomplete picture at best and might even lead to incorrect conclusions.

Conversely, an assembly line seller does not face the same constraints and can employ a wide variety of comparative statistics that compare the efficacy of sales professionals against a statistically established norm. By examining hundreds of different data points, sellers can now drill down and discover what makes an individual salesperson successful and which professionals are following the ideal path.

Armed with this information, sales assembly line sellers are able to hone in and take targeted corrective action where necessary. Consider the following two examples:

For the environment in our first example, one of the best performance indicators is "close rate." The close rate can be defined in many different ways, but here it is the ratio of deals closed to appointments performed by a salesperson. This statistic shows whether each professional is working every lead appropriately and not "big-game hunting" or cherry-picking through leads. Conversely, straight quota only makes a dollar evaluation and does not provide insight on whether opportunities are being wasted.

In the web-meeting sales assembly line environment, however, where the leads are passed on to the salespeople from the lead-generation professionals, there is a higher tendency for the salesperson to "dump" prospects (i.e., send them back to lead generation without performing the scheduled appointment) that do not seem attractive, since they did not spend the effort identifying the lead and because another lead will be provided in short order. However, from the seller's perspective, dumping a lead is extremely wasteful, as it costs the company money to obtain the scheduled appointment. Therefore, it is critical to use the demo-performed statistic, which is the ratio of appointments performed to appointments distributed to sales from inside sales. In situations where the perform rate is substantially lower than the norm, the corresponding salesperson may not be taking full advantage of the largess that the seller is providing, and as such, is not optimizing the sales opportunity presented.

Process Evaluation Statistics

As important as it is to evaluate the performance of the sales professional, it is equally critical to ensure that the sales assembly line is functioning efficiently and effectively. To do so, the system that controls the sales process must collect and analyze a wide range of operating data. This information can be used in two different ways. The first is simply to determine how the system is functioning and whether it is doing so at the optimal level as determined by management. This is relatively straightforward to accomplish. For example, if the seller has determined that each direct sales professional should receive thirty new prospects, the sales system should be able to generate a report that provides management with the actual number of leads that have been passed on from the sales development group. Depending on the complexity of the sales system, there might be hundreds of process figures that provide valuable insight into the operation.

While it is certainly necessary to evaluate the line's efficiency, it is more exciting to analyze the data statistically to determine whether certain actions within the sales process lead to a better sales result. An important tool that sellers can use to determine what works and what does not is a method of statistical analysis known as randomized testing. Randomized testing can be used on historical data. For example, if the leads originating from an advertisement in a trade journal close at a higher rate than the leads closing from a mailing list, it might make sense for the seller to concentrate more money on advertising. However, historical testing is not always accurate because it is difficult to control for other variables in the sales process.

A much better and more accurate approach for the seller to intervene in the market is by running randomized experiments known as A/B tests. This is a powerful technique where the sales system basically "flips a coin" and treats prospects that come up as "heads" differently than the ones that come up as "tails." If the sample size is large enough, which should not be an issue in a sales assembly line environment, each sample group should be statistically identical to one another. This means that any change in the sales outcome is most likely caused by a different treatment of the prospect.

For example, a seller might test the impact of a call script when trying to generate appointments. In this case, the system would randomly assign "call script A" to some telemarketers and "call script B" to other callers. By comparing the average appointment schedule rate, the seller would be able to determine the impact and effectiveness of each call script. The possibilities of what can be tested using randomization are almost endless, and in almost any case, the seller can use the derived information to interact with his or her prospects and customers in a dramatically more profitable manner.

Predictive Statistics

While randomized experiments are powerful, the holy grail of statistical analysis is the ability to predict an outcome based on past results. Predicting the future may seem the stuff of science fiction, but it turns out that by analyzing sales data, sellers do not need to be clairvoyant to figure out what is likely to happen and what actions they should take in response to the expected event. To predict, sellers simply need to take the data generated from their internal sales systems and massage it to tease out the hidden relationships among the various types of information.

A simple form of the approach has always been used in the sales environment. When salespeople forecast results, their usual guidepost is past performance. While past performance is an indicator of what sales the territory *can* generate, it does not indicate what any territory might or should generate at any given point in time. This distinction is important because it is common practice to lowball forecast numbers to ensure that the sales team is able to make their number rather than present an optimal number.

Without using sophisticated statistical techniques, the forecasting can become more accurate by examining the data generated from the environment. For example, the seller might calculate the propensity of each salesperson and the sales team to be overly optimistic or overly pessimistic and then apply this figure to the stated forecast amount to get a more accurate picture of the potential sales opportunity. Another forecasting approach might be to create a specialized formula made up of the various performance indicators generated by the sales process. At CrossBorder Solutions, we employed a complex variation of the basic formula below, with phenomenal results.

Number of Sales Professionals × Number of Appointments × Average Price × Close Rate = Gross Revenue

With this equation, other factors considered included product, sales cycle, size of company, type of salesperson, and industry. This basic approach also could be used to predict a variety of other outcomes mathematically, such as appointment flow and renewal rates.

This approach is relatively straightforward to model, as there is a direct correlation between the different data points and the outcome. However, statistics can be much more powerful when used to uncover buried relationships. To determine such conclusions, statisticians rely on regression analysis, a procedure that takes raw historical data and estimates how various causal factors influence a single variable of interest in the future. What makes this type of prediction engine so powerful is its ability to report how precisely it was able to predict the outcome. Not only does it tell the user the precision of the regression equation as a whole, but it also estimates the impact of each individual factor in the regression equation.

The ability to plug data into an equation and get a measured prediction can change the way sellers interact with prospects and customers. For example, a seller could run a regression analysis to predict which prospects might close. To do so, the equation might consider a wide number of disparate data points, such as lead history, lead source, and the buyer's age, sex, title, and buying history, as well as the time of appointment, type of appointment, number of appointments, the sales professional involved, the sales engineer involved, pricing, offer specifics, timing, and other factors. Taking this data, the statistician would be in the position to predict the chance the prospect will close and become a customer. Furthermore, the seller would learn how precise this prediction was and which factors were driving the buying decision. Armed with this information, the salesperson might approach a sale differently to improve the chances the prospect will close. The possibilities are endless, with the only boundaries being the imagination of the person developing the formula when they are determining which variables should and should not be included in the analysis, and of course, the quality and quantity of the data from which the analysis is derived.

Statistic Examples

The following subset of statistics for the sales function helps evaluate the individual sales professional, the sales teams, and the sales group as a whole. The statistics would be determined by each product for various time periods, including day, week, quarter, and year.

Distribution of Opportunities

Number/percent of opportunities in each sales stage

Number/percent of opportunities in each time stage

Appointment Rates

Number of first appointments scheduled by inside sales

Number/percent of first appointments performed

Number/percent of first appointments canceled

Advances/Retreats for Performed Appointments

Number/percent of leads discarded at close of each stage

Number/percent of leads put on hold at close of each stage

Number/percent of leads advancing at close of each stage

Sales Cycle

Average number of days in each stage
Cumulative average number of days in each stage

Calling Activity

Average/total number of calls processed
Average/total number of calls completed
Average/total number of reaches
Average/total number of advances

Timeliness

Number/percent of tasks performed at each period
Cumulative number of tasks performed at each period
Number/percent of tasks performed on time
Number/percent of tasks performed late
Number/percent of tasks not performed or completed

Appointments Performed

Number/percent of appointments performed
Number/percent of appointments not performed but rescheduled
Number/percent of appointments not performed
and not rescheduled
Number/percent of appointments sent back to inside sales
Number/percent of each performance outcome for all
completed appointments
Number/percent of each reason for nonperformance
Number/percent of appointments qualified
Number/percent of appointments not qualified
Number/percent of opportunities with second appointments
Number/percent of opportunities with three or more appointments

Appointment-Keeping Behavior

Number of first appointments performed as scheduled by inside sales

Number of first appointments performed as rescheduled in conjunction with prospect

Number of first appointments performed as rescheduled by inside sales calling again

Workload

Number of tasks performed across multiple instances of same type of period

Total number of tasks performed for a period

Close Characteristics

Number/percent of appointments scheduled

Number/percent of appointments performed

Appointment-perform rate

Close rate

Total dollars closed

Average price

Total sales cycle

Average sales cycle

Average time in each stage of sales cycle

Average time from first appointment

Percent of quota

Number/percent of closed opportunities with one appointment

Number/percent of closed opportunities with two appointments

Number/percent of closed opportunities with three or more appointments

6. CONCLUSION

An undercapitalized seller can win the Gorilla Game by building and employing a sales approach that relies on web-meeting software. However, this cannot be done successfully by simply swapping web meetings for in-person appointments and telling the sales professionals to work more leads. Instead, for a seller to be successful, the organization must discard many of the long-held beliefs that have been used to run sales organizations in the past and replace them with an entirely new way of thinking about B2B sales. Luckily, sellers now have a guidepost in this journey.

Specifically, sellers can examine how traditional manufacturers overcame the shortfalls of craftsman production and were able to ramp up production and profits dramatically at the beginning of the industrial revolution. By adopting many of the same underlying principles, B2B sellers can build a sales assembly line. By using techniques such as labor specialization, sellers now have the ability to transform themselves into money-making sales machines that can conquer mass markets in an extremely profitable manner.

CHAPTER 6

Running an Optimized Sales Assembly Line

THE PREVIOUS CHAPTERS PROVIDED YOU with an understanding of how a web-meeting sales assembly line can help a technology company win the Gorilla Game. They also explored the inner workings of the sales approach so sellers will have a road map to follow as they transform their operation, while avoiding many of the pitfalls they might encounter. This chapter builds upon this general knowledge base and provides detailed information on a number of important topics (each corresponding to a major module of the assembly line) that will enable web-meeting sales assembly line sellers to optimize their approach.

1. CONQUERING THE LEAD PLATEAU

A web-meeting sales assembly line is a high-volume sales operation. If properly optimized, this type of sales approach will allow a single sales development representative to process approximately eight thousand leads and to generate 720 appointments per year, about seven times more than in a traditional sales operation.

If the seller is lucky enough to target a marketplace with hundreds of thousands of potential prospects, then even though the sales assembly line uses a high throughput approach, the seller likely will not run out of leads. This may not be the case, however, if the seller is servicing a smaller market.

LEADS PLATEAU

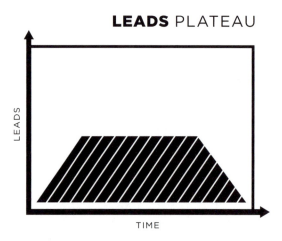

Unfortunately for companies in this latter situation, the lead database that supplies the assembly line with raw leads will eventually reach a plateau and become "tired." All of a sudden, the sales development close rate will begin to drop. This occurs when a majority of the prospects in the database have been dealt with in some way or another. If the sales development effort was optimized, probably most have been reached by the team and have decided not to look at the solution being sold. While raw or untouched potential leads might still exist in the database, they are likely few and far between and have not been reached because they are unreachable! Moreover, there may not be enough of them to keep the assembly line functioning in an optimal manner. Somehow, the seller must find a way to continue to feed the sales beast!

Not having enough leads to keep the sales assembly line functioning is a scary occurrence that can have an enormous negative impact on the entire sales team and the company as a whole. One way to rectify this situation is to launch a totally new, updated product, which will provide the sales team with something fresh to sell. However, this is certainly not a short-term solution to protect the flow of leads through the sales system. A number of short-term strategies can help the company out of this predicament.

Strategy One: Work with What You've Got

The first and perhaps easiest solution is to rework the leads that have already been called. This strategy can take a number of forms. First, the team should ensure that each lead has been called an appropriate number of times. Remember, persistence is key in a high-velocity environment. When trying to reach a prospect, each lead should be dialed up between six and eight times before it is discarded. If this has not been done, it is a great way to ramp up the lead flow quickly. If it has been done, the next pool of leads to rework will be the ones that have been discarded.

Typically, leads are used up and thrown away for one of five reasons: (1) the prospect answers and is simply not interested for any number of reasons (e.g., the product is too expensive, features are missing, they use a competitor's product, etc.); (2) nobody ever answers the phone and the call limit is reached; (3) a gatekeeper consistently blocks the caller from reaching the prospect; (4) the prospect no longer exists, whether this is because the company was sold or the listed contact is no longer employed with the company; or (5) the prospect took a demonstration of the product but decided not to move forward with the product or service.

The first thing the seller can do is to recycle the leads that are in the "not answered" category. While the yield will be pretty low, it is relatively easy to work through this pool once again. However, attempts to reach each prospect should be made only one or two times before giving up. Second, the company can take the "not interested" pool and parse out the different reasons why prospects have passed on seeing a demonstration of the product. Armed with this understanding, outbound marketing campaigns can target these pools of leads with specialized offers or messages that counteract the prospects' hesitancy to view the solution. Third, strategies can be used to work around gatekeepers, such as scheduling calls at off-hours. However, this strategy is unlikely to result in a large increase of positive calls, as normally this pool is relatively small.

Finally, the best recycle approach is for the seller to rework the leads that previously took a demo of the product but decided not to move forward with the solution. Even with a healthy close rate, approximately 80 to 85 percent of the companies passed on the solution and might be willing to consider the solution anew. Again, one way to handle these prospects is to target them with a specialized marketing campaign that highlights their past pain points and how the current solution can meet their needs.

Strategy Two: Offering Enhancement

Once the above strategies have been attempted and lead flow is still suppressed, the seller needs to pursue more aggressive strategies. One approach that will help push the offering up and through the demand curve is to add product features over the course of a product's life cycle. Adding features often can encourage prospects that were unwilling to initially look at the product or even those that actually considered the solution to reconsider their decision.

While adding features will certainly boost demand, any increase in appointment flow and revenue tends to be incremental rather than a true pathway to rejuvenate an entire database. This is because it is likely that each additional feature will only be attractive to a relatively small slice of the marketplace. In addition, in today's business environment, continuous product enhancements are expected, and they do not always generate a great deal of excitement in the marketplace. This is especially the case when the enhancements are matched by competitors.

If the seller can discover an enhancement to the product or service that is a true game changer, though, then this could be something that can dramatically recharge the database. At CrossBorder Solutions, the company developed a feature that made the software radically more powerful and easier to use. As luck would have it, the underlying structure of the competitor's product at the time did not support implementing a complementary feature. This allowed us to go back through the database and schedule a massive number of appointments with companies that had previously passed on the solution.

Strategy Three: Breakaway Enhancements

While adding features will not always create substantial new demand for a product, the counterintuitive strategy of stripping a feature out of the product and marketing it as a stand-alone offering can dramatically increase appointment flow. Under this positioning approach, instead of the old adage that "more is better," the seller can strip away product attributes so the offering solves a single, defined need in the marketplace. This "new" and likely cheaper product can then be sold along its own, newly created demand curve composed of buyers looking to solve a smaller, well-defined problem.

The main product at CrossBorder Solutions contained a feature that allowed its users to update a past analysis automatically. When appointments began to slow for its flagship offering, the company broke the update feature out of the main product and marketed it as a stand-alone offering, appropriately named CrossBorder Update. This relatively simple development effort (we simply turned off pieces of the interface) created a brand-new product category unmatched by our competitors and much cheaper to purchase than the full product solution. This strategy generated an enormous number of new appointments with buyers who simply wanted to update an analysis rather than create a new analysis.

What was even more exciting about this strategy was that it was a Trojan horse for our original product. Our sales team was able to convince approximately 50 percent of the companies that signed up to look at the Update product to consider the full-featured, more expensive product. This had the impact of moving the original product backward into the growth position on the product demand curve while still creating a brand-new curve for the "newish" product.

Strategy Four: Product Rebrand

Sometimes it is simply not possible to find any new names in the database, add new features to an offering, or strip features away to create a new offering. Yet, the seller still needs a way to keep the appointment flow from what has become a stale database. When all else fails, the seller can consider rebranding the product. Rebranding strategies include changing the look and feel of the product or even changing the name of the offering. While these types of cosmetic changes are fairly easy to pull off, they can have a dramatic impact on the seller's ability to keep the line moving optimally.

At CrossBorder Solutions, when appointments started to lag seriously for its flagship product, the company changed its name from CrossBorder PricePoint to CrossBorder Compliance. In addition, it updated the user interface and revamped the associated marketing collateral. While these changes were relatively inexpensive to produce, they had an immediate impact on appointment flow, sales, and revenue. Prospects who had looked at the product before were willing to take another look at the "new" and "improved" offering. Similarly, a sizable number of prospects initially resistant to reviewing the Price-Point product were now interested in checking out the Compliance offering—mostly because of the new name! A solely cosmetic rebrand moved the product back along the demand curve.

Conclusion

Leads are the lifeblood of a sales assembly line. In most markets, a seller will eventually reach what is called a lead plateau, which is where the majority of companies in the market have considered the product. Once this occurs, the lead flow will precipitously fall, and it will become increasingly difficult to feed the sales beast that has been created. That said, a number of time-tested strategies can be employed to help the seller move the product backward along the demand curve or even create a new curve without undertaking an expensive development effort. These strategies can buy the seller time to develop a true new version of the product or identify a new market to attack and conquer.

2. INCORPORATING A/B TESTING

> "One accurate measurement is worth more than
> a thousand expert opinions."
>
> —ADMIRAL GRACE HOPPER

Decision making in sales has long been guided by the proverbial "gut call." Traditionally, the approaches used by sales teams when dealing with prospects have been dictated by the highest-paid person's opinion (HIPPO). Unfortunately, as has been shown time and again, implementing ideas using the HIPPO method is completely, 100 percent unreliable. There are simply too many variables at play for any one person to comprehend what truly makes a prospect move forward with a solution.

With this limitation in mind, the ability to determine what drives a sales decision scientifically has long been thought to be the holy grail for sales professionals and marketers alike. Myriads of companies have begun to examine how artificial intelligence and big data can be used to generate insights on a prospect's purchasing behavior in a B2B sales transaction. In the past, this effort has centered around the general idea of lead scoring. This is where various forms of predictive analytics are used to evaluate the willingness or propensity of the prospect to consider the solution. The main purpose of this process is to align the sales professional's time with the most viable prospects, which should help raise the close rate of the seller.

The principal reason these efforts have focused on the buyer side of the sales equation is that the traditional sales force structure has not enabled sales organizations to evaluate their operations scientifically. Specifically, the fact that most sales professionals operate as Generalists in territories makes it difficult, if not impossible, for a sales organization to isolate and analyze the impact of any aspect of the sales process. Simply too many variables are at work to develop a reliable cause-and-effect analysis. This inability has been magnified by the technology solutions currently offered by sales automation or CRM vendors. Almost all of these packages allow for a degree of free-form data entry, which provides the user with a great deal of flexibility as to what is recorded in each interaction with a prospect. Again, this makes any reliable data analysis practically impossible. Finally, due to the relatively low volume of a traditional sales operation, any analysis of the seller's actions would likely not be statistically significant, even if it could be measured somehow.

A web-meeting sales assembly line does not necessarily suffer from these shortcomings. First, because of its underlying nature, this sales approach is a high-volume operation that should provide enough impressions to make assumptions with a high degree of confidence or certainty. Second, by eliminating territories and pursuing sales specialization, it is possible to equalize the activities of each professional, which makes it possible to analyze their actions effectively. Finally, an optimized process will allow for the accurate capture of a wide variety of sales-related information. This data can be used in innumerable ways to analyze the operation's effectiveness statistically, and, more important, to tease out hidden relationships between the seller's actions and the prospect's response to those inputs.

One of the most powerful ways to evaluate ideas in a scientific manner is to employ a controlled experiment known as A/B testing. In the simplest manifestation of such an experiment, subjects are randomly assigned to one of two variants: (1) the control, which is commonly the existing version of the item being tested, and (2) the variation, which is usually a new version being evaluated. The performance of each variant is then evaluated and measured using a wide variety of key performance indicators. If the experiment was designed and executed properly, the only thing that should drive the difference in the end result between the two options is the change between the control and variation.

Traditionally, in the technology arena, A/B testing is a technique that web developers have used with great success to test variations of a website design. Under this approach, different versions of a web page are tested to see how they influence visitor engagement or buying behavior.

Earlier in this book, an overview was provided on how A/B testing can be employed in the sales assembly line environment. By testing many aspects of the sales process, a seller is able to discern what works and what does not work by examining the behavior of prospects during the sales process. By relying on statistically proven facts,

A/B testing is a powerful decision-making tool that can dramatically improve sales results. This section will now explore this critical concept in greater detail. Specifically, it will outline a detailed methodology that can be used as a strong foundation when implementing an effective A/B testing program in the sales assembly line environment.

THE A/B TESTING CYCLE

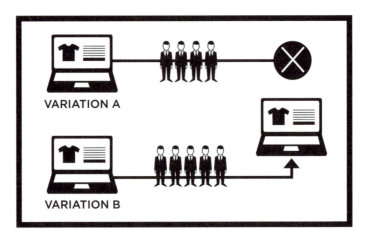

Advantages of A/B Testing

As was shown above, to conquer the mass market, a seller cannot hope to acquire enough customers by simply focusing on sales throughput. Instead, it also must focus on improving the close rate of the sales organization. Only when both of these factors are optimized will a seller be able to achieve profitability and the market leadership position. A/B testing provides the assembly line seller a method to discover myriad ways to improve the close rate of the organization. In addition, pursuing an A/B testing program provides other major advantages.

Promoting Predictive Analytics within the Organization. The HIPPO approach to decision making is indelibly ingrained in the sales culture of most sellers. Data-driven decision making is relatively foreign to many sales professionals, so the results tend to be viewed with a great deal of suspicion and trepidation. A/B testing provides clear outcomes that are easily understandable and are less likely to be met with skepticism. As such, the sales team will likely be more receptive to using various forms of predictive analytics.

Quicker Decision Making. In today's sales environment, it is an indisputable fact of life that everything happens more quickly. To be successful, sellers need to adapt immediately to changes in the marketplace in which they operate. As such, decision cycles need to be extremely short if an organization is going to be successful in the Gorilla Game. Due to its nature, A/B testing allows sales teams to have an immediate understanding of what is influencing buying decisions and then to make decisions in real time on how to adapt to the changing landscape.

While A/B testing is incredibly powerful, it does have significant limitations that must be kept in mind. For instance, an A/B test can only confirm a hypothesis and will not automatically allow the seller to determine what is driving sales behavior. In a similar vein, it is important to note that the test will only show what is better between two possible choices. The fact that one version is better does not mean that this is the optimized option. In addition, although an A/B test will provide the seller with whichever version is working better, the test does not provide the tester with information on why the version was more successful. This lack of insight is not only frustrating, but it reduces the ability of the organization to make systematic changes to take advantage of the perceived insight. Finally, the seller must understand that A/B testing in the sales environment, unlike simply using website optimization, involves human behavior, which can negatively impact reliability even if controls are put into place that try and minimize the role of the team's actions.

Implementing an A/B Testing Methodology

Developing a rigorous and methodological framework is critically important if you wish to obtain reliable and meaningful results from an A/B testing program. This section highlights the various steps necessary to take when implementing a program.

A/B TESTING OPTIMIZATION STRATEGY

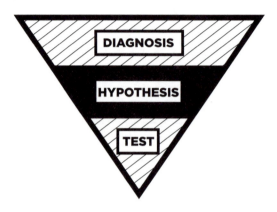

Step One: Define Goals. The first step is to determine the primary goals behind the A/B test and how success is defined. Are the A/B tests being run simply to understand the impact of one testing item on the close rate, or is the company trying to improve the overall functionality of the sales assembly line? The more complex the testing, the greater the importance in following rigorous testing methodology.

Step Two: Develop the Testing Hypothesis. To develop a properly formulated testing hypothesis, it is first necessary to identify a problem in one aspect of the sales process that you wish to solve, along with the suspected causes of the issue. Next, you need to determine a possible solution to the problem in question. Finally, you need to make an educated guess about the expected result and link this result to the key performance indicator (KPI) that you wish to measure. For example, if the identified problem is a low sales development close rate when dealing with CFOs, which you suspect is due to the message being put forth, a valid hypothesis might be changing the message to discuss how the solution will impact the financials of the entire company and increase the number of appointments with CFO targets. Though there is nothing to prevent the measurement of several indicators during a test, it is important to identify a primary KPI to differentiate between the variations. It is not rare, in fact, to observe a test that affects two KPIs in opposing ways (e.g., an increase in the close rate but a decrease in the callback rate).

Step Three: Prioritize the Identified Tests. Likely the first two steps will have brought numerous issues to light, and various testing hypotheses will have now been formulated. Next, it is necessary to develop an overall testing schedule. When deciding a testing order, it is strongly recommended to focus on items that are relatively easy to test and that will provide quick wins that enhance the credibility and demonstrate the power of the solution to the sales team. Once this has been accomplished, it will be much easier to obtain buy-in from the sales professionals involved in the testing process, which is critical, due to their involvement in the process. At the end of the prioritization exercise, a testing schedule should be developed and shared with the entire sales organization so they view themselves as full participants in the testing program.

Step Four: Implement the Actual Test. In general, a testing program will encompass the following actions:

- **Determine the Data Source and Test Time.** The first step to implementing a reliable A/B test is to ensure the analysis can achieve a sufficiently high statistical confidence level. Confidence level indicates how much faith the testers can have in their estimates. For published works in peer review journals, a confidence threshold of 95 percent is normally required. However, when examining the impact of marketing actions, an 80 percent threshold is often satisfactory. The confidence degree is primarily based on the number of impressions measured. For example, in the sales development arena, it would be dependent on the number of dials made and the positive reach rate. In addition, timing also must be taken into account. Specifically, to improve the confidence level, consider allowing the test to proceed over several days to take into account the idea that prospects can behave differently on different days of the week. Of course, until the threshold is reached, any conclusions are suspect.

- **Random Distribution of Sales Assets.** It is critical that the prospects from the selected lead source are randomly and *equally* divided among the sales professionals.

- **Random Distribution of the Control and Variation.** Equally important is to ensure that each professional is randomly and equally given sales assets that are either the control or the variation when interacting with the prospect.

- **Ensure Test Program Compliance.** Unlike a website that is undergoing A/B testing where the system tracks the visitor's interaction with the site, A/B testing in the sales environment depends 100 percent on the various sales professionals complying with the instructions surrounding the test. Therefore, it is critical that management carefully monitor how each professional interacts with the sales asset to ensure the test is being conducted as planned.

- **Analyze the Test Results.** Once the test runs its course, it is critical that there be a mechanism in place that provides in-depth data on the test that was conducted. For example, when running an A/B on an SDR script, the report should indicate how many overall conversations were conducted, the number of conversations where each of the variants were employed, and the close rate of each.

Step Five: Communicate the Test Results. After an A/B test is completed, at a bare minimum it is essential to let everyone that was involved in the test to learn the results of the experiment. This will positively influence future buy-in to the testing process and help ensure that future tests are embraced by the sales organization.

Step Six: Implement the Winning Version. If the test discovers that a variation is performing better than the control, the new version should be rolled out and implemented on the sales assembly line. Once the change has been put into production, it should be continuously monitored to ensure that the long-term results are in line with expectations.

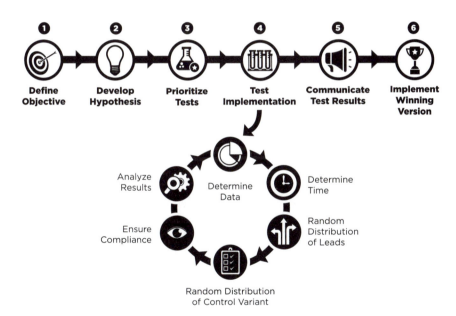

Which Elements to Test

This is a recurring question, one that relates directly to the fact that, in many cases, businesses are unable to explain their close rate—be it good or bad. Each case is therefore different, and the aim of this chapter is not to provide an exhaustive list of elements of the sales process to test but rather some of the broad categories to consider. Of course, you can specialize in one aspect of the process, but market-leading close rates can be achieved by mastering each category.

- **Sales Development Script Analysis.** The script the sales development professionals use when making an outbound cold call or answering an inbound lead can have a dramatic impact on the outcome of the call. Different types of buyers, as categorized by title, role, gender, company size, and industry, will respond differently to different messages. A/B testing provides the ability to test various hypotheses concerning the presentation of the solution being sold. For example, some questions that might be asked include:

  - What format and structure should the call follow?
  - What primary marketing message or value proposition should be employed?
  - What type of information is provided and at what level of detail?

- **Sales Development Offer Analysis.** How the value proposition is communicated to the prospect can have an enormous impact on the close rate of the sales development professionals. Hypotheses that can be examined include:

  - How should pricing questions be handled?
  - What price should be presented based on the type of buyer?
  - What promotional offers are most effective and how should they be conveyed?

- **Sales Development Call Cadence Analysis.** Simply having SDRs cold-call prospects over and over again is not the optimal way to obtain appointments. Too many of the prospects ignore the phone calls and are eventually discarded as unreachable. It has been shown that by interspersing outbound cold calls with emails and voice mail messages, an SDR team can dramatically improve their contact and close rates. Calling cadences or the pattern to which the calls, emails, and voice mails are left should be customized by campaign and persona. That being said, it is important to A/B each cadence to achieve optimal results. Items that can be tested include:

  ○ The actual pattern of calls, emails, and voice mails
  ○ The subject line and body of the emails
  ○ The message and actual wording of each voice mail

- **Marketing Collateral Analysis.** Direct marketing efforts can have a dramatic impact on inbound and outbound lead generation. There are numerous opportunities in this area to hypothesize how the different campaigns can be used to generate positive response rates, reach rates, and close rates for the solution being sold, including:

  ○ Who is the target of the piece?
  ○ What is the design and general look and feel of each marketing piece?
  ○ Is one type of direct marketing more powerful than others?
  ○ What is the overall message of each piece, including how the value proposition is communicated and the level of information provided?
  ○ How is the marketing piece worded?
  ○ What promotional offers work best?
  ○ Is it helpful to include a prominent call to action?

- **Other Sales Development Processes.** How the sales development group functions in relation to the prospect can also have an outsize influence on the close rate of the sales development team. Areas that might be explored in an A/B test include:

  - Will scheduling a callback at a specified time and date be helpful? Does the time period matter?
  - Does a phone call or an email work better in reminding a prospect of an upcoming scheduled demonstration?

- **Sales Demo Performance.** How the solution is demonstrated to the client using web-meeting software can have a dramatic impact on the close rate and price achieved. Different types of buyers as categorized by title, role, gender, company size, and industry will respond differently to various approaches. A/B testing provides the ability to test various hypotheses concerning how the solution being sold is presented. For example, some questions that might be investigated include:

  - What format should the demo follow?
  - What information should be included in the PowerPoint presentation?
  - How detailed should the product demo be? Should it be customized for the prospect?
  - What role should the sales engineer play?

- **Sales Offer Analysis.** While the sales professional is moving the opportunity through the sales funnel, a number of hypotheses can be tested, including:

  - What optimal price can be charged while maintaining a target close rate?
  - What does the actual offer entail and what is the best structure for the deal?

- How should the offer be presented?
- What is the best way to follow up on an offer?
- Which special inducements work best to propel the opportunity to move forward?
- What impact does the sales engineer have on the closing process?

Every web-meeting sales assembly line seller is different, so the aim of the above section was not to provide an exhaustive list of elements to test but rather some of the aspects to consider. In any event, by allowing the seller to implement an A/B testing program on the sales development and sales processes, businesses will be in the position for the first time to understand and articulate their close rate, be it good or bad. With this heightened awareness, the value proposition of the seller's solution and understanding of why prospects move forward or do not will become much clearer. Thus, the sales assembly line seller will be in the position to manipulate every aspect of its interaction with each buyer, thereby optimizing the results of the sales process.

WHAT CAN YOU TEST?

OFFERS
Discover which deal terms drive sales

PRICE
Find out the impact of raising price

SCRIPTS
Uncover which message works best

MARKETING COLLATERAL
Discover which approach generates more leads

PROCESSES
Ascertain which actions drive results

DEMOS
Learn which style is more convincing

62%

38%

Efficient A/B Testing Tips

Below is a short list of best practices that will enable businesses to avoid common pitfalls associated with A/B testing programs.

Test One Variable. By testing only one variable at a time, the impact on the variable will be better isolated. If more than one variable is modified simultaneously, it will be impossible to identify which change produced the effect observed.

Run One Test. It is not unusual to be tempted to run several tests simultaneously, especially when there are clear indications that the results can help the seller drive revenue. Resist this temptation! It is advisable to run only one test at a time. Results will be difficult to interpret if two tests are running in parallel on the same group of prospects.

Ensure Statistical Reliability. It is not advisable to make any decision at all until the test has achieved a level of statistical reliability of at least 80 percent, but 95 percent would be ideal. The probability that the differences observed in the results will be due to chance rather than to the modifications introduced will be too high otherwise.

Measure Multiple Indicators. Before launching an A/B test, it is important to establish a primary KPI, such as close rate, that will be used to determine the test outcome. That being said, it is sometimes illuminating to measure multiple KPIs, which will provide deeper insight of the results. Among the secondary indicators often measured are positive call rate, reach rate, average dials per completed calls, and callback rate.

Reduce Outside Influences. External variables can have a strong impact on A/B testing results. For example, running a test during the close of a monthly or quarterly sales cycle will likely influence the sales professional's approach to prospects. Therefore, it is preferable to limit these collateral effects by ensuring tests do not coincide with known outside influences.

Reduce Internal Sales Bias. One of the largest obstacles to adopting

A/B testing within a sales organization is internal resistance from the line professionals. Whether this is deliberate, concealed, or even unconscious, many sales professionals believe that sales is an art, not a science, and as such, team members often do not see the value of the A/B testing. Without buy-in, this can damage the testing process simply because these naysayers might not religiously follow testing protocols. One of the best ways to reduce institutional resistance is to report the results of tests and the possible gains in sales revenue to the entire team. As these improvements should positively impact each sales professional's pocketbook, once the process is proven, the practice should become addictive.

Conclusion

This gives you a general awareness of factors that must be considered when implementing an A/B testing program in the sales environment. A successful program requires more than just a testing tool. Instead, the success or failure of the program will depend largely on whether the tester follows a strict testing methodology or regime and every effort is made to buy into the various stakeholders in the process. This advice should provide some insight as to how a sales assembly line seller can establish the right foundations from the outset. From experience, we know the first tests are decisive in terms of generating and sustaining interest in testing within the business.

While A/B testing is certainly time consuming, we firmly believe the effort is worth it and will result in higher close rates and therefore a significantly larger number of customers being acquired.

3. WHERE DOES SALES DEVELOPMENT BELONG?

One of the most frequently asked questions concerning a sales assembly line is how the sales development group should be structured.

Specifically, where in the organization should the team be located and how should the relationship between the sales development and sales representatives be optimized? While the final answer to both questions is somewhat dependent on the product being sold and the culture of the organization, there are a number of factors that should be considered in making these two important decisions.

Sales development is a function that does not have a clear home. Since it is critical to the success of the sales operation, it seems reasonable and logical that the group should report to the sales department. However, on closer inspection of its primary role, which is to generate interest in the product or service being sold, perhaps the group best belongs to the marketing department. In this section we will examine the pros and cons of each option.

Should Sales Development Report to Marketing?

In the traditional sales environment, marketing is responsible for building awareness for the products and services being sold while the sales Generalist is responsible for scheduling his or her sales appointments. Having a "wall" between the two groups makes a great deal of sense and serves the needs of both groups. From marketing's perspective, not having an active role in lead generation means that it can focus its efforts on "soft" activities that are difficult to measure and evaluate. From the sales group's point of view, the Generalist presumably knows how many leads he or she needs on a monthly basis, and as this is relatively few, it is better to do the work independently than to risk having an interloper involved in the group's daily affairs.

In many organizations, the role of marketing has undergone what might be considered a sea change. As the Generalist model has lost favor, in a bid to increase sales throughput, marketing groups are often tasked with the role of generating qualified leads for the sales

MARKETING MODEL

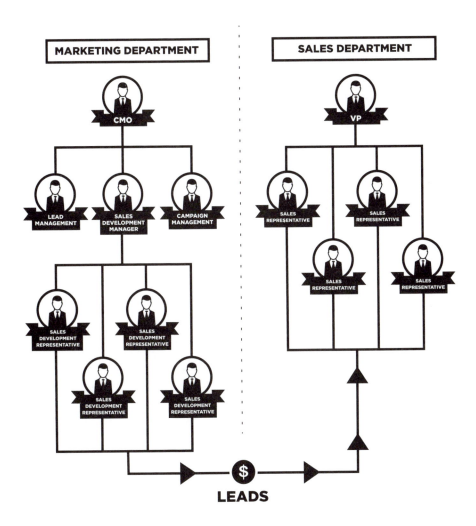

team to work. In fact, according to the Bridge Group, 24 percent of sales development groups report directly to marketing. There are a number of benefits and drawbacks to this approach. Following are some of the pros:

- **Reduction of Operational Influence.** In most organizations, the sales group is a powerful force that is used to getting its own way. Removing the sales development function from the group's purview makes it a lot less likely that they will be able to negatively influence the lead-generation operation. For example, sales representatives typically only want leads that are perfectly qualified. However, as it is often difficult, if not impossible, to obtain this level of insight, it often makes sense for the sales development team to provide the sales team with any lead that shows an interest, with the hope that the account executive can use their amazing powers of persuasion to transform a lukewarm lead into an opportunity that might close. Therefore, placing the sales development function into the marketing group will often maximize the overall number of leads generated.

- **Tighter Control of the Marketing Message.** It is likely that the marketing group is responsible for developing the message, the cadence, and even sometimes the script employed by the sales development representatives to convince the prospect to move forward with a demonstration of the product being sold. If the callers are part of the sales group, they might be less likely to "stay on message." Being part of the marketing group helps ensure the right message is given at the right time. This is especially the case when A/B testing campaigns are undertaken and the results are 100 percent dependent on the sales development representative religiously following the directions in the testing environment.

- **Tighter Coordination with Direct Marketing.** We have seen how the sales development close rates can improve substantially by immediately following up direct marketing actions with targeted phone calls. This process tends to work more efficiently when the callers are part of the organization that actually sent out the marketing piece.

- **Marketing Knowledge.** Especially in the case of inbound leads, it is likely that the prospect is calling as a response to a particular marketing action developed by the marketing team. When sales development representatives are part of the marketing group, it stands to reason that they will be more familiar with the marketing materials, such as e-books or white papers, which will allow them to have a more fruitful conversation with the prospect.

There are also significant cons to having the sales development function be part of the marketing group:

- **Deprioritization of Lead Generation.** Marketing's primary job in most organizations is to build awareness of the solution being sold through direct or indirect marketing campaigns. Their performance is most often evaluated by using some objective measure, such as website hits, downloads, or even the number of inbound leads generated. When they are given the new responsibility of sales development, often this task takes a backseat or plays a smaller role than their more traditional functions. This, of course, can lower overall productivity.

- **Inferior Training.** At the end of the day, lead generation is a form of selling. The caller needs to convince a prospect, who is often initially unreceptive, to sit through a demonstration of the product or service. Most successful sales professionals have mastered this all-important skill and would presumably be an important training resource to the callers who are often young and inexperienced. Removing sales development from the sales department makes this important training opportunity more difficult to accomplish, which can lower overall productivity.

- **Lack of a Career Pathway.** Sales development is often the first step sales professionals take as they begin their careers. Placing the group in the marketing department makes it more difficult to move the professional "up" as he or she becomes more proficient. Moreover, the lack of a clear pathway makes it more difficult to attract sales candidates in the first place.

- **Lead Distribution Headaches.** Unless technology is being used to automate the hand-off of opportunities from sales development to sales (and vice versa in rescheduling situations), hand-offs between departments are ripe for trouble. It is extremely difficult to ensure that leads do not get mistakenly dropped or misplaced.

- **Increased Departmental Rivalries.** Normally, there is an institutional rivalry between the marketing and sales groups. Placing the lead-generation function in the marketing department can certainly increase tensions, especially if the sales department views this action as an "infringement" on its turf. In addition, it provides the sales department with a built-in scapegoat if sales goals are not met, as it is convenient to claim that numbers were missed because of a lack of qualified, high-quality leads.

Should Sales Development Report to Sales?

It should come as no surprise that there are similar arguments that can be made to keep the sales development function in the sales group. The pros for this approach include the following:

- **Improved Training.** Where there is a tight relationship between the sales development and sales team, it is likely that the sales skills of the sales development representatives will dramatically improve, which should lead to a higher close rate.

- **Clear Career Pathway.** Since most sales development representatives will be future sales professionals, putting the callers into

SALES MODEL

MARKETING DEPARTMENT

CMO

LEAD MANAGEMENT

CAMPAIGN MANAGEMENT

SALES DEPARTMENT

VP SALES

SALES DEVELOPMENT REPRESENTATIVE

SALES DEVELOPMENT PROFESSIONAL

SALES DEVELOPMENT PROFESSIONAL

SALES DEVELOPMENT PROFESSIONAL

SALES DEVELOPMENT PROFESSIONAL

SALES PROFESSIONAL

SALES PROFESSIONAL

SALES PROFESSIONAL

SALES PROFESSIONAL

LEADS

$

the sales group provides a more seamless transition to different sales roles within the organization.

- **Lead Distribution.** The hand-off of prospects from sales development to sales when they are in the same group is apt to be more efficient and effective.

- **Tighter Coordination.** Having both groups report to the same management structure allows for tighter coordination of sales policies, procedures, and tactics.

- **Elimination of the Blame Game.** Having the two groups together effectively eliminates the blame game that often occurs when expected sales numbers are not achieved. It is difficult, if not impossible, for people in sales management to blame anyone but themselves when sales numbers are not achieved.

Again, there are also significant cons to having the lead-generation function be part of the sales group:

- **Lack of Checks and Balances.** When lead generation is separate from the sales department, there is no check on the actions of the sales group and its professionals. Greater insularity can quickly lead to inefficient and even ineffective processes.

- **Too Much Power.** It is risky to have so much power and responsibility in the hands of one group and likely one manager. If that professional were ever to leave, not only would sales be impacted but so would the lead-generation function.

- **Undue Influence.** Having the two groups together enhances the ability of the sales professionals to encourage the sales development representatives to cherry-pick their calls and focus their efforts on bigger and better names, which almost always leads to a decreased appointment flow and lower sales volume.

- **Ineffective Marketing Campaigns.** Not only will the sales development representatives be less familiar with the various marketing campaigns, but it is extremely difficult to ensure that the callers stay on message. While this can be harmful from an overall perspective, the lack of tight control completely eliminates the ability of the team to perform accurate A/B testing of the sales development process.

- **Minimization of Sales Development Professionals.** When the sales development team is housed within the sales group, it is not unusual for the callers to begin to focus their efforts on helping the sales professionals close more deals rather than finding new opportunities. Remember, they want to be sales professionals and likely do not need much encouragement to get involved with the actual sales process rather than simply finding prospects and passing them on. In fact, it is not unusual for sales professionals to begin to view the sales development team as junior sales assistants who perform menial tasks for the sales professionals. Of course, this negatively impacts the sales development productivity.

In spite of the above, data from the Bridge Group shows that approximately 73 percent of sales development representatives report up to the VP of sales. Perhaps this is one of the reasons the inside sales approach does not work as well as expected or hoped.

At CrossBorder Solutions, originally the two groups were kept together within the sales division. This was primarily done to reduce costs, as we believed it was cost prohibitive to hire two senior managers, and it was more cost efficient to have the VP of sales control the entire process. However, as the sales development team grew, the downsides of having this all-important function report to sales became problematic. The sales development professionals wanted to only call well-known companies or schedule appointments for prospects that were perfectly qualified. The marketing group was also having difficulty making them stay on message, as they believed they knew what worked best with prospects.

As such, the sales development team was moved and placed under the purview of the marketing team. Many steps were taken to eliminate some of the problems associated with this approach. For instance, although the group was part of the marketing function, a senior sales professional was placed in charge of the group, which helped to ensure they were properly onboarded and received continuous high-level training. Second, outbound calling was prioritized by tying the compensation of the marketing leadership team to appointment volume.

Group Structure

A second question that often arises is whether sales development professionals should be teamed with sales professionals. Under this structure, the caller obtains appointments and ensures they go off for an assigned salesperson. There are many benefits to this approach:

- Since the sales professional lives or dies by the success or failure of the sales development representatives, there is a fairly high probability that the salesperson will take an active role in training and supervising the caller.

- Teaming a sales development professional with a sales professional helps make the caller feel like an integral component to the sales process and the sales team. In fact, the callers truly tend to enjoy spending time with the sales professionals and learning from them. As these team members often want to become salespeople in the future, this not only helps attract these professionals to the organization but also helps retain them as well.

- Under the team approach, the salesperson has on tap one or more professionals that have formed a positive relationship with the prospect. Moreover, these individuals are presumably proficient in dealing with these leads. As such, they can truly help the sales professional close more business.

- As most CRM products have the capability to team callers with salespeople, it makes the overall lead-distribution process more efficient and effective.

While the above reasons are certainly worthy of consideration, there are many negatives associated with a team-based structure:

- If the sales development professional is incompetent or his or her performance is subpar, the performance of the sales professional can be significantly degraded through no fault of his or her own.

- The team approach makes the statistical analysis of the performance of both the sales development and sales professional much more difficult because an additional important uncontrolled variable has been added to the mix.

- Inevitably, personnel conflicts will develop. In most cases, except for the most egregious, the sales professional will prevail due to his or her revenue-generation role. This second-class status can negatively impact morale and performance of the sales development professionals.

- If a sales development professional leaves the company, the associated sales professional can suffer a significant loss of earning potential through no fault of his or her own.

- If a sales development professional leaves the company, the revenue goals of the entire company can be negatively impacted, as the entire sales team is now underproductive.

- The sales professional will need to spend time training and working with the sales development representatives, which will negatively impact throughput.

- Whatever work the sales development representatives do to assist the sales professional in closing deals will be at the detriment to the overall appointment-generation goals.

- The sales professional will almost always influence the sales development professionals to get "better" appointments. This will result in lower appointment volume and lower sales because it is next to impossible to predetermine with any degree of accuracy which prospect is more likely to close.

For the above reasons, using a team approach is strongly discouraged when seeking to optimize the web-meeting sales assembly line. Leads that are obtained by the sales development team should be distributed using an algorithm that ensures statistical equality. The simplest way to accomplish this is to use a standard round-robin approach. However, to ensure that the prospect's time constraints are taken into account, it is often important to consider which sales representative is available at any given time and then equalize appointment flow in another manner. This approach not only ensures statistical equality, which enables the sales organization to evaluate performance better, but it also improves overall throughput.

4. DEALING WITH MULTIPLE PRODUCTS

In a traditional territory-based sales environment where the salesperson travels to meet with the prospect, it is an absolute no-brainer to have the same sales professional sell multiple products. This dramatically lowers the cost of sale and raises the overall close rate associated with each prospect. In a web-meeting sales assembly line environment, where territories are superfluous and the sales professional never meets with the prospect face-to-face, the answer of how an enterprise should handle multiple products becomes much less clear. At the extremes, there are basically two options. One is where the entire sales development and sales team sell multiple products. At the opposite end of the spectrum is the situation where a new assembly line is built for each product being sold. To illustrate the pros and cons of both approaches, consider the situation where a new product is launched alongside an existing offering. First, let's examine the positives of having the *same* team attempt to sell both products:

- It is significantly quicker and easier to ramp up appointment production and to make actual sales for the new product when existing, well-trained, and proven professionals are employed.

- It dramatically lowers the expense and therefore the risk of the product launch, since new professionals do not have to be hired.

- Initial feedback from the marketplace is more reliable, since the existing sales team presumably has an established track record and can be trusted.

- The close rate for the sales development and sales team should be significantly higher because experienced, battle-tested professionals are being employed. Moreover, in the case where the same target is the buyer for both products, there is a greater chance that one of the solutions will be attractive to the prospect, which improves the overall close rate.

- As a new product launch is typically an exciting milestone, providing existing professionals with the opportunity to sell the new offering improves morale and job satisfaction and also reduces the tedium of the job.

On the other hand, there are several cons to using the same assembly line to sell multiple products:

- Human nature will lead the sales team members to pitch and sell the product they understand better. As a result, the new product will often be given short shrift (if it is mentioned at all), which can give the impression to management that the product is not being well received in the marketplace.

- Because sales professionals make most decisions with their wallets in mind, the team will naturally focus its efforts on the product that has a higher close rate. Often, this means that one offering will be pushed to the detriment of the other product. As new offerings often have a lower close rate in the early stages of the product launch, this generally means sales professionals will continue to push the old product to the detriment of the new product. This perpetuates the lower close rate and makes it less likely to achieve takeoff velocity for the new product.

- In a perfect world, the salesperson would try to sell both products at the same time, as this should increase the overall close rate associated with the prospect rather than the product. However, introducing two products often makes the sales process more complex, so the salesperson normally will use intuition to pick one product to lead with. Since this decision is made with imperfect information, the close rate of both products might suffer.

- Selling the same product over and over again can be tedious, and sales professionals might prefer to sell the new product just because it is something different and exciting. This is especially the case if the new product has a reasonably high close rate or is selling for a higher price. This can dramatically lower the sales volume of the existing product line. A decrease in predictable revenue can put the seller in an unfortunate position.

- Typically, it will be much easier for the sales development team to schedule appointments for the new product, especially if the lead database of the existing product is becoming "stale." This could result in sales of the existing product stalling before the new product proves viable as to its close rate and price. Once again, this can hurt the financial position of the seller.

Presumably, the decision to launch a new product was primarily made to develop a second revenue stream. For the above reasons, this is unlikely to occur, as the revenue from one product will simply replace the revenue from another product. An alternative approach is to develop a second assembly line to handle the sales of the new product. Using the same fact pattern described above, the positives associated with this approach are described below:

- Separate sales development and sales teams mean the professionals will give each offering their full and undivided attention.

- The sales professionals will aggressively attack the new market, since their compensation structure will be based entirely on the success or failure of the new product launch.

- Relatively more calls will be made and more appointments will occur. This will provide the seller with valuable market feedback in a relatively short amount of time, which can be used to fine-tune the sales offerings and improve the new product's close rate.

- The higher volume of sales calls will mean that a reliable statistical analysis can be completed on the operation earlier in the sales process, which will improve the close rate in a quicker fashion.

- Any revenue achieved through sales of the new product will be additive in nature.

- The higher volume of sales appointments should allow the seller to maximize the presented opportunity, which is especially important if the seller is a first mover within the marketplace.

However, consider the cons associated with this approach:

- Building a new sales assembly line with all of its associated stages is difficult and time consuming, which can slow the introduction of the new product to the marketplace.

- Constructing a new assembly line can be an expensive proposition, which increases the risk of the new product launch.

- Hiring qualified sales professionals for the new line can be difficult, as the new product being sold does not have an established track record.

- The close rate of the sales development and sales teams will be dramatically lower due to the fact that the product and the sales team are new.

- Unless sophisticated software is used, it is difficult to manage two assembly lines where both products are being sold to the same buyer. The chance for collisions is extremely high, which can negatively impact both new and existing deals by lengthening sales cycles and lowering close rates.

At CrossBorder Solutions, after much thought and argument, the company decided to build out a full assembly line for each new product it sold. This was in spite of the fact that the company's products were sold to the same buyer within the same department, which dramatically increased the likelihood of collisions. It was also financially burdensome at a time when there were many other demands on the capital accounts of the company. However, management believed it was simply too risky to pursue a shared assembly line strategy. The company had just spent over $5 million on the development effort of its new product and it was not willing to leave its success or failure in the hands of the line sales professionals. As a result, the company created a new assembly line to maximize the new sales effort. To help ensure the new product would have the best chance for success, the new assembly line was seeded with two sales development and sales professionals from the existing line. While there was a slight negative impact on the existing product line, it was significantly lessened by simply increasing the appointment flow of the remaining sales professionals.

5. BUILDING CUSTOMER RELATIONSHIPS

In a traditional SaaS environment, most companies have chosen to forgo significant up-front revenue to rent their software on an annual basis, in an attempt to build an ongoing, recurrent revenue stream. If managed correctly, over a number of years, this recurring revenue stream will hopefully dwarf what a company could have achieved under a perpetual license scheme. As such, the company's valuation is primarily based on the success or failure of the resulting renewal revenue. Valuation aside, though, it is doubtful that the new sales operation is generating enough profitable revenue to keep the organization's head above water, especially if one of the traditional sales methods is being employed! As such, it is an understatement to say renewals are critical to the traditional SaaS organization.

In spite of the critical nature of renewals, the underlying structure of a traditional SaaS company prevents its renewal operation from being as effective or efficient as possible for the following reasons:

- In most organizations, the salesperson who closed the account is the professional who manages the customer relationship and is responsible for the renewal revenue. A salesperson who is an effective Hunter of new sales accounts does not normally have the right personality to coddle clients effectively. This will likely lower the renewal close rate.

- Hunters will typically focus their time and efforts primarily on new sales opportunities. In most situations, the individual sales professional will be better off closing a new sale than losing a renewal sale. As a result, renewals are often given short shrift again, thereby lowering the close rate.

- The amount and quality of time spent working with the client to ensure ongoing success are directly proportionate to the stickiness of the solution being sold. For example, a software solution that is fully implemented and integral to the customer's success or failure will make it difficult for the customer to replace the solution with one from another vendor. In that case, as the solution is sticky, the sales professional responsible for the renewal will likely spend the bare minimum of time and effort with this client.

- If the solution is easily replaceable, the salesperson will spend more time working with the customer but only at the bare minimum necessary to guarantee the renewal and his or her commission. Taken from a transaction perspective, the salesperson has absolutely no incentive to do anything more!

- To prevent the sales professional from totally ignoring renewals, it is likely that the seller is paying the same commission rate to the salesperson for renewals and new sales. This means the organization is paying too much. A renewal sale is much easier to make than a new sale and can be done by a less experienced sales professional. Therefore, renewal sales should be compensated at a much lower rate.

- When the salesperson spends time on renewals, it takes time away from working on new sales opportunities. As new sales throughput is one of the most important gating factors in the profitability of the enterprise, anything that lowers this number is ineffective and inefficient.

Renewal Sales in the Web-Meeting Sales Assembly Line Environment

At first glance, it would be natural to assume that a sales assembly line seller would be less dependent on renewal revenue due to the new sales volume that can be achieved. Nothing could be further from the truth. Besides, from the impact on the seller's financials and valuation, customer retention serves an even more important purpose in this sales environment. Due to the incredible throughput of a sales assembly line, a seller needs more than six times as many references as a traditional seller requires! To put it in perspective, if a traditional salesperson has five leads that need two references each, the traditional sales operation professional will need to supply ten references, assuming the same name is not used more than once.

Contrast this to the sales assembly line environment, where the same professional would need two references each for thirty prospects for a grand total of sixty references per salesperson per month! To get this many customers who would be willing to pick up the phone and speak positively about the solution being sold on a monthly basis, the sales assembly line seller obviously needs a huge cadre of customers that are fanatic supporters of the company.

Therefore, in the sales assembly line environment, happy customers who are willing to serve as references are a critical raw material for the sales assembly line. Without this valuable commodity, the line will not function efficiently, and the overall close rate will fall. It is critically important that everything under the seller's control be done to ensure that their customers are insanely satisfied with the solution they have licensed.

Luckily, for the web-meeting sales assembly line seller, the assembly line concept has many attributes that will help the enterprise achieve this goal. Specifically, by breaking off the customer-management function from the salesperson, the company is able to obtain several benefits from labor specialization:

- The seller is able to hire experts at building relationships and coddling clients.

- Since the customer success professionals' primary responsibility is to build tight customer relationships, they can spend significantly more time making sure that every client is happy with the solution.

- By spending all their time supporting clients, the customer success professionals quickly become functional experts.

- The increase in profitability due to the lower commission payments provides the seller with more flexibility in designing programs that enhance close rates.

Taken together, these form the foundation for the web-meeting sales assembly line seller to ensure an adequate reference supply!

Becoming a Customer-Centric Sales Assembly Line Organization

Unfortunately, simply breaking off the customer success operation from sales as part of the labor specialization effort is not enough to ensure that the seller will have enough happy clients who will be willing to serve as references for the sales team. This is only a first step, which provides the framework for possible success. Instead, the typical technology company must undergo a fundamental transformation. All too often, enterprises believe if they have the best product with the most features, prospects will descend on them like locusts and then remain as customers with the company forever. In today's business environment, where product differentiation is often fleeting, nothing would be further from the truth. This is especially the case in the time period before a market leader is chosen.

Therefore, the company must transform itself from being a product-centric organization (i.e., one that primarily relies on the product feature set to keep its customers happy) into a customer-centric company (i.e., an enterprise where the customer, not the product itself, is the most important priority). In a customer-centric environment, customers are the center of the universe, and everything revolves around them. By becoming a customer-centric seller, the sales assembly line enterprise will be able to build the loyalty necessary to guarantee a steady supply of references for the sales team. To make a successful transition, it is helpful to follow several key principles.

Build Long-Term Relationships with Clients. The key to building this type of loyalty is to develop unique and personal relationships with every client. Once relationships are established with customers, they become friends with the customer service professionals in the sense of someone who comes to trust them and enjoys speaking with them. The key to such a relationship is for the customer success professional to get to know customers better—way better—than a traditional customer. By carefully and intently listening to the customer during the sales process, the professional should be in the position to know everything about the client. At CrossBorder Solutions, our customer success professionals knew the nickname, wife or husband's names, kids' names, vacation spots, schools, birthdays, anniversaries, and hobbies of every client. Basically, anything they were willing to share, we wanted to know! By understanding our customers in every way possible, we were able to exceed their expectations consistently.

Clearly, building this type of deep relationship with thousands of clients is not easily done, especially in the sales assembly line environment where the primary mode of interaction with the client is over the phone or via web meetings. To accomplish it, every effort should be made to touch the client on a regular basis and then draw him or her out in conversation. At CrossBorder Solutions, our internal sales system ensured that every client was called and *reached* at least once per month just to say hello and to check how things were going. During implementations, it was not unusual to check in daily to ensure that everything was going as planned. Moreover, if a client had an issue, our customer success team immediately followed up a day later to make sure everything was resolved properly. In fact, monthly client touches were key performance indicators for our customer success professionals.

The client at some point will probably want to meet in person with someone in the organization. However, at CrossBorder Solutions it was our policy never to have our professionals go on-site. This was not a monetary-based decision, but one that was made to ensure that the professionals' other clients were not shortchanged by their absence from the office. Instead, to accommodate our customers' wishes, the company regularly brought our customers to our office. We flew them in at our expense, put them up at a hotel, took them out for dinner, and of course, worked with them on their specific product issue, whether it be training, implementation work, or other areas. This program was an amazing way to build tight relationships with our clients. Not only was our customer success staff able to interact with each client, but it also provided senior management with the opportunity to touch the client. After spending two days at our office together, we were able to make friends for life.

Regularly Exceed Expectations. Once the customer success professional has gathered this type of knowledge on each customer, it should be his or her goal to exceed the customer's expectations at every touchpoint. In today's business environment, with so many automated and impersonal interactions, it is not hard to wow the clients with a little bit of extra effort. These efforts do not have to be expensive or elaborate, as customers appreciate small indications of care. At CrossBorder Solutions, we had a list of "hugs" we regularly provided to our clients, which included:

- Handwritten thank-you notes from the salesperson

- Birthday cards

- Anniversary cards

- Tickets to shows and sporting events

- Five-minute callback rule, even on weekends and after hours

We went the extra mile to thank super references—clients who were willing to take more than twenty reference phone calls per month. Each quarter, the company invited our super references to an all-inclusive trip to a resort. In addition to providing them with a continuing education opportunity, the trip provided us with a chance to get to know our customers and their families in depth and to let them know how passionate we were about earning their trust and loyalty.

All Hands on Deck. It is not enough to have customer success professionals play this role alone. To be a truly customer-centric organization, the organization needs to make sure that everyone has a singular focus on ensuring customers' success with the licensed solution. To facilitate this mind-set throughout the organization, it is critical that senior management regularly touches the clients, as this sets an indelible example the rest of the organization feeds upon. At CrossBorder Solutions, this process started the moment the prospect became a client. Within twenty-four hours, I would send a handwritten note, thanking the clients for their trust and letting them know that we would do anything in our power to earn their loyalty. I also included my home phone and cell phone numbers in the note, so I could be reached at any time if they needed to talk to me.

This policy extended past the management team. Everyone at CrossBorder Solutions, even the finance and development professionals, took turns helping with client implementations so they would understand what our customers were experiencing. We also had a monthly contest to see who in the organization could provide the craziest level of customer support. The winner would get an actual straitjacket and a $200 dinner with his or her significant other.

This led to some amazing stories, such as when one of our clients was pulling an all-nighter to prepare for an IRS audit the next morning. Without asking permission from management or charging the client, a professional services associate drove five hours and worked through the night with the client to ensure he was ready. Of course, he also picked up Dunkin' Donuts and coffee on the way. This company became a client for life. Not only did the client become a super, super reference, but the client was the first to line up to renew and license new products as well as do what they could to help the company succeed.

Another great example is of one of our larger clients, located in downtown New York City on 9/11. Due to the attack, their building became uninhabitable. When our customer success manager for the client heard this, she immediately called the client's VP-Tax on her cell phone and invited their entire tax department to work out of our offices in SoHo for as long as necessary. Again, this Fortune 100 company became a customer for life.

6. CONCLUSION

For a traditional SaaS technology company, it is simply good sense to build a loyal customer base. Having happy clients will help the company to generate predictable ongoing revenue, which is extremely valuable, especially if the new sales operation operates at a loss. It also stands to reason that satisfied clients will license more products and pay for additional services. Most traditional software companies provide just enough support, no more and no less, to ensure that this occurs.

In the sales assembly line environment, this is not enough. Due to the new sales volume associated with this sales approach, the sales team needs an enormous number of clients who are willing to serve as enthusiastic references for the company. Without these references, the assembly line will slow, and close rates will dramatically fall. Since references are a vital raw material to the sales process, a sales assembly line seller must do everything in its power to become a customer-centric organization. This is a mind-set in which everything the company does is to further the customer's goals. Whether it is writing notes, paying for visits, or doing things traditional software companies would never consider doing, building strong relationships is critical to ensuring that the seller meets its new sales and renewal sales goals.

CHAPTER 7

Final Thoughts

I RECENTLY HAD DINNER WITH four old friends. Each of them is now a successful venture capitalist located in New York City. The group gets together once per quarter to catch up and discuss potential deals. Over the past few years, these conversations have been relatively upbeat. Money has been flowing nicely and valuations have been steadily rising. However, the mood that night was decidedly subdued.

The previous week had been particularly brutal for the stock market, with a drop of over 10 percent. Moreover, the never-ending talk of a possible recession had everyone on edge. The discussion that night primarily centered on the impact these economic reverberations would have on their portfolio companies. A story in *The New York Times* that day, about the number of potential "unicorns" that were going to be in serious trouble if valuations continued to nosedive, had made the group uneasy. Everyone was noticeably worried about their portfolio companies—especially the ones having difficulty gaining traction in the marketplace.

Eventually, the discussion turned to why so many of these companies were not hyperscaling. The general consensus around the table was that the "founders" simply did not have the management chops to get the job done. Clearly, if valuations continued to fall, the unemployment line was going to get a little bit longer with all of the CEOs about to be replaced with professional managers that could possibly help these fledging companies weather the incoming storm. At one point in the conversation, I said, "It's not the CEOs' fault." It got very quiet and everyone looked at me. Being a former CEO, I believe the expectation was that I was going to defend my brethren and perhaps blame my friends for making bad investment decisions.

Instead of launching into a soliloquy on whether the business community truly needed another e-commerce website, I told them flat out that their issue was not with their CEOs. The problem was largely centered on how their portfolio companies were selling, or not selling, their products into the marketplace. My dinner partners had heard this from me before, but on this night it seemed that the current economic environment finally made them pay a little closer attention. Once again, I patiently explained:

In any technology market, only one company will dominate any given marketspace. This company, called the Marketplace Gorilla, will garner 50 percent of the market's revenue and 75 percent of the profits. Except for one or two other enterprises, most of the other market participants will struggle to survive and will eventually fail entirely.

The seller that can achieve a 40 percent market share first will be victorious in this winner-takes-all game. The deciding factor is often not which company has the best technology or was first to market. Instead, it is the company that can sell dramatically more than the other market participants.

A Marketplace Gorilla will often be anointed within the first four to six years of the creation of the market category. This limited time frame means that companies that want to compete to win the Gorilla Game must hyperscale their sales operations.

In most cases, it is mathematically impossible for a company that is relying on a direct sales approach to become a Marketplace

Gorilla. This sales methodology will simply not allow the seller to acquire enough customers in the required time frame.

As few of my dinner companions' portfolio companies were on the path to become gorillas, this harsh reality meant they were not going to realize the necessary gains that would allow them to generate an acceptable rate of return for their limited partners. With this scary fact, it is no wonder everyone looked so crestfallen.

One of my friends pointed out that he and the other investors at the table had heeded my earlier advice and many of their portfolio companies had transformed themselves into "inside sales" sellers, complete with specialized lead-generation teams and salespeople who used web-meeting software to interact with prospects. While I applauded him for taking what amounted to baby steps in the right direction, I let him know, in no uncertain terms, that this was not going to be the hoped-for panacea.

While an inside sales company would lose a little less money and probably gain approximately 30 percent more clients, basic mathematics dictated that this limited changeover would *not* normally enable the seller to reach enough prospects to conquer the mass market. This is because the company's sales throughput is still too low and its associated close rate will likely have fallen, sometimes fairly dramatically. I asked my dinner companions if any of their portfolio companies that had made this shift to the inside sales model were now throwing off so much money that they no longer needed follow-on financing or were closing thousands of new deals per year. No one raised a hand. The silence said it all too clearly.

As I went into my standard stump speech detailing my reasoning, I could not help wondering how, in 2016, business sellers were largely in the same position they had been in twenty years ago. With all of the advancements in technology and business processes, how could companies be selling in much the same manner as they did at the turn of the century? While it is fashionable to blame the sales traditionalists who might automatically resist any change, this is clearly not the only reason most sellers are stuck in such a destructive cycle of failure. After all, other business functions have had the same type of stalwarts, and they were pushed aside in the relentless drive to achieve efficiency and effectiveness.

Instead, much of the blame needs to be leveled directly at the CRM industry. By focusing their efforts on building cloud-based systems primarily designed to help traveling salespeople work more efficiently, they missed the opportunity to reimagine the basic structure of B2B sales. As such, today's B2B sellers, if they want to use a CRM system, have for all practical purposes been forced to use sales methods that have been proven time and time again to be unsuccessful for a large majority of their users in the technology space. Often, this is the common failure denominator and is certainly one of the drivers behind the troubling failure rate of technology concerns.

After providing my friends with this upsetting news, I figured I would offer them some new advice, based on recent research that has been conducted on the gorilla phenomenon. When making an investment into a technology concern, an institutional investor should understand the following:

1. An investor who is considering buying into a company that operates in a marketspace where there is already an established Marketplace Gorilla should give strong consideration to passing on the opportunity, as the company will almost never generate an acceptable compounded rate of return. The only exception to this is where the company is offering a discontinuous innovation that could possibly usurp the underlying market structure.

2. An investor who is considering buying into a company that operates in a market where a leader has *not* been established, but the company under consideration is not acquiring nor has the

ability to acquire a sizable percentage of the market's potential customers each year, should give strong consideration to passing on the opportunity. This is because the company will likely not become the Marketplace Gorilla, and as such it will almost never generate an acceptable compounded rate of return. As an extension, if the potential portfolio company is using a traditional sales methodology, the investor should probably run the other way.

3. If an existing portfolio company operates in a market where there is an established Marketplace Gorilla, the investor should divest his holdings at the earliest possible point in time, as history has shown that the company's valuation will begin to fall precipitously as the market leader's position becomes better solidified. Unfortunately, this portfolio company will almost never generate an acceptable compounded rate of return.

4. Company founders and employees who are making an investment with their time and effort are in the same unfortunate position as the institutional investors. This is especially the case if they are counting on their stock options being worth something someday.

I wanted to leave off on a good note, so I let everyone know that not all was lost. As long as a Marketplace Gorilla had not yet been anointed, then likely there was still the opportunity for a company to be successful in any given market as long as it was willing to adopt a radically new sales approach. In recent years, innovative, forward-looking companies have learned that the secret to hyperscaling is to build high-velocity sales assembly lines. By using many of the same techniques that traditional manufacturers employ, including labor specialization, repeatable best practices, and specialized technology, sellers can mass-produce sales for a fraction of the traditional cost. In fact, it costs so little to establish a sales assembly line, B2B sellers will no longer need the enormous amounts of funding necessary to reach takeoff velocity.

If the process is optimized properly through the use of big data analytics and artificial intelligence, it should be possible for a sales assembly line seller to double the close rate and achieve up to an eightfold increase in sales volume. This combination serves as a customer acquisition multiplier that will allow the company to project a sales footprint many times larger than its marketplace competitors that are using traditional sales methodologies. This powerful method of force projection can serve as a catalyst that can propel the seller to become the Marketplace Gorilla and realize all the spoils of the war.

In conclusion, as outside financing continues to tighten, B2B sellers will be forced to reexamine their underlying sales approach in an attempt to stave off disaster. As potential failure is the best impetus to try new things, it is my expectation that more and more B2B sellers will adopt the basic tenets of this sales approach in full. Moreover, as more companies choose to become sales assembly line sellers, it is likely that technology solutions will be created to meet the needs of this new marketplace. Of course, this will then encourage and allow other companies to make the necessary transition. It is my hope that this book will add to the overall discussion of this category and will encourage companies to employ this amazing, game-changing approach to business sales.

The History of Gorillas
in the Marketplace

THE MARKETPLACE GORILLA CONCEPT WAS first espoused in the early 1990s by Jeff Tarter, a leading technology industry analyst and the editor-in-chief of the influential newsletter *Softletter*. He proposed that in any technology market, one company would eventually become the market leader, and this enterprise would be supported by one or perhaps two other strong competitors. His views were built upon the writings of Jack Trout and Al Ries in their best-selling book *Positioning: The Battle for Your Mind*. The authors put forth the position that becoming the market leader was critically important, as this company would eventually get twice the long-term revenue of the second-place finisher and four times as much as the third-place competitor. Moreover, except for one or two competitors, "most me-too products fail to achieve reasonable sales goals" and will eventually fail. In the book *The 22 Immutable Laws of Marketing*, they proposed that every market eventually "becomes a two-horse race" and that the "number one law of marketing was that it was critically important to become the market leader!"

Geoffrey Moore, in *Crossing the Chasm* and *Inside the Tornado*, further expanded on this basic concept. He, too, believed that one company, what he called the Gorilla, would eventually dominate any given technology market. Out of the other market participants, one or two companies would become "Chimpanzees," who are "candidate Gorillas that didn't get picked by the market," but they survived by playing the "role of a kinder, gentler Gorilla." Finally, furthering the primate scenario, he believed there would be a number of monkeys who would feed off any market excess with a strategy based on the concept of selling me-too or cloned products for a cheap price. They would have a niche role in the market as long as "demand exceeded supply." While this doesn't sound at all enviable, it's a better result than that achieved by most other market participants, who would eventually fail.

Specifically, in a follow-up book called *The Gorilla Game*, he wrote about the long-term competitive advantages of being the Gorilla:

———

"Gorillas get more customers because they attract better press coverage than their competitors and they get premium treatment from sales channels looking to maximize sales. In addition, Gorillas attract potential partners who are interested in having access to the market leading company."

———

"Gorillas can raise barriers to market entry by making subtle changes in its technology. Over the longer term, it will thus become more expensive for customers to switch to competing standards. Therefore, Gorillas can successfully keep more customers."

———

"Gorillas can use economies of scale to continuously
drive their costs down. They can even force their
partners to bear the major portion of enhancement
development costs by outsourcing low-added-value
work to third parties."

———

"The Gorilla's products can be priced at a premium
because they are the industry standard. In other words,
a Gorilla can keep its profits high while competitors
are forced to offer discounts simply to offset the fact
they are not the industry standard."

Due to this advantage, Gorillas eventually obtain 50 percent of the market revenue and 75 percent of the profits from any given market. This marketplace dynamic has been borne out by countless technology enterprises. In most mature marketspaces, a Gorilla has been anointed and this company has received a majority of the bananas. As companies such as Salesforce.com, Intel, Microsoft, Google, Marketo, and others can attest, it is good to be the Gorilla! From these works, it became an entrenched truism among venture capitalists and entrepreneurs that there can be only one Gorilla in any technology marketplace. Yet up until quite recently, this concept had been borne primarily by observation but had never been proven with actual data in an empirical, scientific manner.

However, this has changed, as recounted in the groundbreaking book *Play Bigger* by Al Ramadan, Dave Peterson, Christopher

Lochhead, and Kevin Maney. In this recently released best seller, the authors examine how technology companies dominate markets by becoming Category Killers—which is their name for the Gorilla concept. In a research report entitled "Time to Market Cap: The New Metric That Matters," they exhaustively examine whether a technology market is a winner-take-all environment or one where there is room for several players to dominate.

Specifically, the authors examined public and private data on more than 500,000 companies and 18,000 private investors that engaged in over 52,000 private M&A deals or VC funding rounds in the technology space since 2000. From this research, they built an extensive model that proved the following conclusions.

- Due to the reduction in costs of distribution and the time/resources necessary to scale, technology companies are growing at a faster pace than ever before. In addition, new products and services get discovered and adopted much quicker than ever before. In fact, they found that Category Kings break out in four to six years, rather than the traditional ten years. The result of this is that "money flows to a few winners more quickly, and away from losers equally as quickly" and the technology market resembles a "high-stakes, winner-take-all poker game."

- Due to the increased speed that companies become market leaders, the data showed that "winners win faster than ever, which means that losers lose faster than ever." This means that execution mistakes are extremely costly and that there is little time for a company to pivot to different strategies. If the technology company has not obtained a market leadership position, it loses its ability to become the Category King and will likely experience shrinking valuations and slowed growth.

- In this accelerated environment, only one company, a Category King, will on average take more than 70 percent of the total available market cap in their space. This leaves little room for the number two, three, and four players. In fact, the study showed "a common phrase in technology, 'There's room in this market for several players,' seems to be utterly false. The data shows that there's room in any well-defined category for one super successful player and a bunch of companies that wind up as category serfs, and those that just die."

While the book offered many other important insights—especially how companies can design categories—the takeaway that can be drawn from their work and the authors that preceded them is that becoming the market leader in a category is critical to the success of the company and should be pursued at all costs.

The Greenhouse Software Sales Assembly Line:

How the Company Has Hyperscaled Its Sales Operation

A Conversation with Marc Jacobs, VP of Sales

THE NEW YORK CITY-BASED GREENHOUSE Software is one of today's fastest growing start-ups. Greenhouse is an SaaS platform designed to help companies make great hires. They have developed a suite of tools for everyone in a company to more effectively source, interview, and collect meaningful feedback about candidates. By having a more structured and data-driven approach, Greenhouse empowers companies to more effectively measure and improve their recruitment process.

The company historically targeted fast-growth companies with less than five thousand employees, but it is now making inroads into larger enterprises. It should be noted they are operating in a very competitive marketspace with over two hundred other enterprises vying for a piece of the recruitment process. That being said, there are approximately ten VC-backed companies currently competing with Greenhouse to become the market leader in this space.

The company has been on a tear and has become one of the darlings of the VC community. It has raised over sixty million dollars from A-tier firms such as Social Capital, Benchmark, and Thrive Capital. Driving this success is the fact that the company has become a hypergrowth SaaS enterprise. In fact, since its founding in 2012, Greenhouse has hyperscaled and has doubled in size every six months. In the past two years, its customer base has grown over 500%.

Public credit for this growth story rightfully goes to Greenhouse's CEO, Daniel Chait. However, Marc Jacobs, the company's VP of sales has been equally responsible for its sales success. When Marc joined the company in 2014, the company had five sales professionals. It now has over seventy and is continuing to grow dramatically to meet market demands. When Marc joined the firm, he worked with Daniel and his director of sales, Aaron Melamed, to implement a high-velocity sales assembly line designed from the start to help the company hyperscale. It should be noted that Marc was VP of sales at CrossBorder Solutions prior to the company's sale to Thomson Reuters. As such, many of the concepts he introduced at Greenhouse have been discussed earlier in the book. Recently, I had the opportunity to sit down with Marc to discuss in detail the sales methodology he has put into place. Below is a summary of our discussion.

When I asked Marc for the secret of his success, he, as expected, immediately gave credit to the hard work of his sales team and how the processes were put into place at Greenhouse to hire the right people and ensure they were successful. One of the keys to accomplishing this success was to implement a high-velocity model based around the concept of sales specialization. He stated, "Specialization was tremendous because it is much more efficient to get each professional to perform his/her task in an optimal manner when all they had to do was focus on a single operation. For example, it was much easier to get an SDR ramped up quickly if their only focus was prospecting." To this end, he built out a multistage sales assembly line based on the following steps or tasks.

MARKETING

While the marketing group produces a wide range of persona-driven content employed by the sales team, it does not have a distinct role on the sales assembly line. While a common discussion in SaaS is whether SDRs report into Sales or Marketing, Marc felt that "sales management was better equipped to train and manage those types of professionals." Furthermore, in fast and growing organizations such as Greenhouse, "It's really important to have a specific career ladder that will allow people to get promoted relatively quickly," and having the sales development professionals report to Sales provides them with a clear promotion path. That being said, Marc stressed that the marketing group is invaluable in ensuring that the sales group has the content necessary to support the customer acquisition effort.

INBOUND LEADS

At Greenhouse, some prospects sign up for a demonstration of the product on the company's website or call in to speak to a representative. These inbound leads are passed directly to the inbound sales development representatives (ISDRs), who work with them to schedule a demonstration by an account executive. A second type of inbound lead are those that enter the sales process because they have downloaded content or attended an event. Often these leads are not looking to make a purchase or to even evaluate the software solution. Historically at Greenhouse, these MQLs would be nurtured by Marketing until they eventually requested a demo. Recently, Greenhouse created a specialized role within the ISDR team called an MQL specialist.

These MQL specialists will leverage the fact that these leads downloaded content and reach out to them or others within the account to try and schedule a demonstration of the product. Approximately 40% of the leads worked by the sales team are inbound; this is a relatively soft number, however, because it is difficult to accurately measure the impact of the content on inbound and outbound leads due to the difficulty of understanding whether the outbound efforts drove the prospect to the website or if something else did.

OUTBOUND LEAD GENERATION

In addition to the inbound leads, Greenhouse also has a team of SDRs responsible for outbound lead generation. The SDRs use a variety of methods to contact potential leads and convince them to schedule an appointment with a sales professional. Because of the ease of email automation tools, the team "became comfortable with more marketing-type activities where they mostly mass-emailed prospects and would only just make an outbound call to respond to any questions or qualify the lead. They really did not need to do a whole lot of—or any—cold calling." However, as the low-hanging fruit disappeared and the automation-type emails stopped working because "buyers were being inundated with all the emails, and they were less likely to open them than they were in the past," Marc and his management team moved to a combination of calls and emails, which entailed measuring a minimum number of calls per day. Interestingly, they have moved away from firm dial numbers, and now management focuses on results, although the number of dials and other activities are the "first thing that they look at when things are not going well."

To improve the conversion rates, the sales development team employs a number of repeatable practices. First, based on the persona of the prospect being called, customized cadences are employed. For example, "On the first try, the SDR makes a call. Then, the second time, they leave a voice mail and an email. The next day, they'll go to LinkedIn and send an inmail, and this process continues until the lead is reached or is deemed unreachable." Below is a sample cadence that SDRs have used at Greenhouse:

Step 1 – Day 1 – Email

Step 2 – Day 2 – Email + Double Dial Call

Step 3 – Day 3 – Email

Step 4 – Day 6 – Email

Step 5 – Day 7 – Call & Value-driven VM

Step 6 – Day 9 – InMail

Step 7 – Day 11 – Email

Step 8 – Day 11 – Double Dial

Step 9 – Day 12 – InMail

Step 10 – Day 14 – VM

Step 11 – Day 14 – Reference VM Email

Step 12 – Day 18 – Diff Value

Step 13 – Day 21 – Follow up of Diff Value

Step 14 – Day 24 – Breakup email

Second, the SDRs use customized scripts that "push a different business value based on the persona that is being called." Making this even more complex is that the team employs customized scripts for different call cadences. Marc mentioned that the "alignment between marketing and sales drives this process, as marketing is responsible for coming up with the messaging used in calls, emails, and voice mails."

Traditionally, the SDR has been responsible for fully qualifying the prospect. To this end, they had a defined list of questions to ask the prospect before it was passed onto the account executive. "In fact, they have specialized it so much that the first time the account executive was speaking to the customer was at the demo." However, Marc stated they are starting to see this is not necessarily the best experience for the customer since "although the SDR is asking really good questions, the account executive inevitably ends up asking many of the same questions." As such, the company has started to test out having the account executive be responsible for qualifying the prospect prior to the demo being performed, after the SDR confirms a minimum qualification to create the opportunity.

Once demos are scheduled, they are passed on to the account executives. Originally, the demonstrations were distributed on a random, round-robin basis without much segmentation. However, the company has now grouped its SDRs and account executives into three categories: small businesses, middle-market, and enterprise. Under this new approach, the SDRs in one category only obtain demonstrations for account executives in a corresponding bucket. This alignment has forced the team to focus on the middle market and enterprise segments rather than focusing only on the small companies where demos were easier to get but the deal size was much smaller. When questioned whether they work as a team, Marc stated, "The teamwork could be much better, but it's not because they are intentionally avoiding working together—but without a smaller number of people aligned together it is very difficult. The plan is to move toward a POD concept where there is a lot more alignment between a small number of SDRs and a small number of account executives in each POD and where it is much more natural for them to work together to help each other and hold each other accountable."

In the future, Marc expects this POD concept to further transition to the point where the PODs are employed to pursue an account-based strategy organized by verticals. "Verticals are better because, by having domain expertise, SDRs and AEs can connect better with the prospect," he stated. "Furthermore, in a web-based environment, where you don't have much face-to-face contact, industry domain expertise can help build more of a personal connection. From a marketing and training perspective, the team can craft specific pitches, better leverage customized content, and most importantly, connect by sharing reference accounts of customers that are in the opportunities domain."

ACCOUNT EXECUTIVES

As described above, the prospect is sent to the account executive and is qualified during the discovery and demonstration. To help ensure the meeting takes place, Greenhouse has automated the reminder process. The SDR who scheduled the demonstration is responsible for reminding the prospect. Marc stated, "By adding that additional step, the demo completion or show-up rate grew." If the demonstration needs to be rescheduled, the SDR account performs that task because "they still have the relationship until the demonstration."

When Marc first started at the company, account executives were performing up to six demonstrations per day. However, he stated, "It was great for them, and they loved doing it. However, the negative aspect was there was no way the account executives could possibly focus enough on the harder sales in their pipeline. They would mostly focus on the things they could close the easiest, which left the other opportunities to fall through the cracks." When asked what the optimal number of demonstrations per day is, Marc feels that "two, maybe three per day would be ideal." Each account executive is supposed to keep "approximately 125 deals in his/her pipeline," Marc stated.

"I wouldn't say we have done a great job on keeping to this limit, but we have made requirements that each account must have human activity within the last thirty days. This forces the AE to either focus on all of their accounts or get rid of accounts that they are not actually working. But again, it's a fine line between having too many and having not enough. However, it also depends on the customer size of the segment. If AEs manage enterprise deals, they shouldn't have more—in my mind—than fifty accounts at any given time. However, if they are working more transactional small business accounts, they can handle 150+. The main factor, though, is that they reach the opportunity at the very least once per month, but it should be a lot more."

The model calls for the demonstrations to be done over the Internet using web-meeting software. If it is a strategic account located in New York City or San Francisco (where Greenhouse has offices), an account executive is encouraged to visit the opportunity, particularly if the customer asks for a meeting, and a face-to-face meeting would move the deal forward. However, Marc stressed face-to-face is the exception, not the rule. Another important role on the sales team is the sales engineer. Marc stated, "I've been at companies where sales engineers' roles included handling most of the demonstration. At Greenhouse, it's not that way. The account executives are responsible for the entire demo. We leverage the sales engineers where it makes sense to take advantage of their technical knowledge. Specifically, they are available to speak with customers to answer deep technical or security concerns. They also add a different type of credibility when speaking with a customer that is either very technical or that brings their IT person into the discussion. As we move toward larger accounts, the sales engineers will absolutely play a larger role earlier in the process."

Marc stated that, unlike the SDRs, the account executives have to have a little more flexibility in their process. That being said, it is important to build in repeatable processes that help ensure consistent sales results. It was important to Marc when he got to Greenhouse to align sales stages with the buying processes of the companies they were selling to. This creates a much better probability of winning and also makes predictability more likely. As he stated:

"It is impossible to be predictable if one person has one definition of proving, which another person has as buying process, and it's the same situation. So what we've done is take out the subjectivity and make it very clear what the exit criteria is for every stage. Before the account executive is allowed to move an opportunity from one stage to the next, the opportunity has to meet the specified criteria. I'll give you an example of this. If they are in the proving stage and we want them to get to our next stage, the closing bucket, they need to demonstrate certain exit criteria. In this case, the account executive has to have confirmed they have the money allocated to make the purchase, and we need a defined timeline of when they are going to move forward. Only if we have positive answers to those questions and this has been confirmed in writing, can the opportunity move to the next stage."

He noted that the further the opportunity moves down the funnel, the tighter the exit criteria becomes. The second repeatable process that leads to a higher close is an extensive training program that allows every account executive to understand the value proposition, how to handle objections, how to price, how to explain pricing, and how to negotiate deal terms. "And then from a demo perspective, they all have been taught to do the demo the same way. While they explain different things in a little bit different way by putting their own twist into it, we make sure they are doing it in a way that is similar. Then if we see someone is struggling, it is easier to see why they are going off-track. For example, they might not be focusing enough on making sure that a pain of the buyer is being addressed properly."

CUSTOMER SUCCESS

Once a deal closes, the opportunity moves to the customer success team. This team of account managers handles the customer journey throughout the term of the contract. This function does not report into Sales, which Marc conceded is unusual. The account managers are solely focused on ensuring that the customer is successful with the solution. However, ninety days prior to the renewal, a specialized sales professional, called a renewal rep, is going to take on the responsibility of renewing the customer. Renewal reps are not compensated on a commission basis, but instead have a base and a variable, and their variable is based on certain goals, which include expansion and low client churn.

Marc noted that this basic model was somewhat problematic, especially in the area of maximizing upsell opportunities. The account managers at Greenhouse were not interested in selling and were not incentivized to do so, either. This was not an issue early on because customer engagement was a huge priority and the company only had one product, which was sold as a company-wide solution. The opportunity to upsell was only coming at renewal time and was limited to a growing customer needing an expanded solution. However, after the company made an acquisition last year, created a new product, and started to sell services, something had to give.

In order to handle this new situation, the least disruptive solution was to get the account executives back in the process to handle any upsells. This is not ideal since the account executives are removed from the relationship when a customer becomes a customer. Greenhouse is evaluating better options for aligning the account manager with selling or adding the renewal manager into the process earlier and giving them upsell responsibility.

KEY PERFORMANCE INDICATORS

Marc and I had a brief discussion about which KPIs he relies on when evaluating the sales development and account executive function. In regard to the former, he stated that while he keeps a close eye on the number of dials each professional makes, the leading indicator he cares about is how many qualified sales opportunities each SDR schedules each month. From the account executive perspective, he looks at a number of indicators. He stated, "If I had to pick one, I would say it is close rate. But we also have started to look carefully at revenue per lead. If I have an account executive who's getting one hundred leads and is generating $100,000, and I have another account executive who is getting the same number of leads and is generating $150,000, that is something we need to know so we can maximize our revenue opportunities."

CONCLUSION

At the end of our conversation, I asked Marc two questions. First, what challenges keep him up at night, and two, what he thinks will be the keys to success on a going-forward basis. The biggest challenge he faces is that "scaling is really hard and getting harder all the time." He went on to lament that, "Once the low-hanging fruit is gone, the question becomes how do you continually drive the sales process forward and attack the remaining market in the best way? We need to have a plan to deal with the constantly changing environment and be ready to change our internal processes to meet these challenges."

In regards to how he is going to accomplish this, as expected he stated, "We will double down on employing sales specialization, as it has given us a tremendous advantage in the marketplace. It has been much easier to get young employees up and running quickly if they can focus on one task. For example, an account executive can be productive much quicker if all they need to learn how to do is demo the product and close business, as opposed to having to worry about marketing, prospecting, and even customer success." He went on to stress that "creating repeatable processes around the hiring of staff has been critical as well. Because we specialize and try to figure out what makes each role successful, it is important to make sure that we find the right people and put them in the right role so they can be successful." Finally, he credited the investment in money and time to ensure that each task has been optimized and that each professional has been given the training and tools necessary to be successful.

**DONALD SCHERER** was the CEO and cofounder of CrossBorder Solutions, one of the world's largest tax software companies. He developed the company's sales assembly line and pioneered the use of web-meeting software to work with prospects and customers. Cross-Border was sold to Thomson Reuters for a home run valuation.

Afterward, Donald founded and is now the CEO of AssemblySales. com. Based on the software that powered CrossBorder's sales operation and the methodology outlined in this book, ASSEMBLY is the first enterprise SaaS solution that has been designed from the ground up to run high-velocity sales assembly lines. By optimizing performance, ASSEMBLY helps B2B sellers hyperscale by mass producing sales. This will allow them to quickly overwhelm their competition and achieve a market leadership position.

Further information on ASSEMBLY can be found at www.Assem-blySales.com and on Twitter @AssemblySales. Follow Donald on Twitter @Donald_Scherer.